AN INTRODUCTION TO BIBLICAL GREEK WORKBOOK

AN INTRODUCTION TO BIBLICAL GREEK WORKBOOK

Dana M. Harris and Chi-ying Wang

ZONDERVAN ACADEMIC

An Introduction to Biblical Greek Workbook

Requests for information should be addressed to:
Zondervan, *3900 Sparks Dr. SE, Grand Rapids, Michigan 49546*

Zondervan titles may be purchased in bulk for educational, business, fundraising, or sales promotional use. For information, please email SpecialMarkets@Zondervan.com.

ISBN 978-0-310-10860-3 (softcover)

ISBN 978-0-310-10861-0 (ebook)

Cover design: LUCAS Art & Design
Cover photo: Dogancan Ozturan / Unsplash
Interior design: Kait Lamphere

Printed in the United States of America

20 21 22 23 24 25 26 27 28 29 30 31 32 /PHP/ 15 14 13 12 11 10 9 8 7 6 5 4 3 2 1

CONTENTS

ACKNOWLEDGMENTS

Writing a textbook, together with this workbook, is never an individual effort. So many people have played important parts, especially a series of graduate assistants and Greek teaching fellows at Trinity Evangelical Divinity School, who have used these materials and helped to refine them considerably. I can only mention a few of these individuals who were particularly helpful in their contributions to this workbook: Geoff Ng, Dave Bryan, Jennifer Guo, and Pancha Yahya. I am also grateful for the wonderful department support that I have received, including but not limited to my department chair, David Pao. I especially thank my coauthor, Chi-ying Wang, whose work on the initial materials for this workbook was invaluable.

The editorial crew at Zondervan Academic, especially Chris Beetham, has been great to work with. This has been very much appreciated on something as technical as a workbook, with so much attention to detail.

Above all, I am thankful to my Lord Jesus Christ, without whom none of this would be possible or would matter.

Dana M. Harris
June 2020

A NOTE TO INSTRUCTORS

One of the priorities of *An Introduction to Biblical Greek Grammar: Elementary Syntax and Linguistics* is to use examples from the GNT rather than constructing phrases to illustrate various syntactic points. In the textbook, this means that sometimes students will see words or forms in an example that they have not yet learned. This has the advantage of exposing them to the actual text of the GNT from the beginning. In this accompanying workbook, however, this approach would cause unnecessary frustration for students, as they would repeatedly encounter items that they had not yet learned. Thus we have modified examples from the GNT for the assigned exercises in the following ways: verb tense-forms have sometimes been changed (e.g., substituting a present tense-form for an aorist tense-form in exercises prior to chapter 10, when the aorist indicative is introduced), words that have been assigned as vocabulary words have sometimes been substituted for the actual words in a given verse if those words have not yet been assigned, and sometimes part of a verse that uses syntax or vocabulary that has not yet been covered has been omitted (indicated by ellipsis points). Additionally, most exercises contain only a portion of what is an entire sentence in the GNT. In no case is the original meaning of the sentence significantly altered by these modifications. In the answer key, where Scripture references are provided, "cf." indicates that a verse has been modified from the original wording. Students are encouraged to look up the actual reference and to compare it with the modified version in the workbook. Finally, a "Pop-Up Lexicon" is provided for many of the exercises, which provides additional vocabulary necessary for completing the exercises. All words that appear in Pop-Up Lexica are also included in the lexicon at the end of the textbook.

In this workbook, Chi-ying Wang tracked down the words for parsing and the examples from the GNT. Dana M. Harris wrote the additional notes. We both worked on modifying the texts for the exercises and adapting GNT passages for the four integration passages.

WELCOME TO THE WORKBOOK!

You should complete these assignments after you have studied the material presented in *An Introduction to Biblical Greek Grammar: Elementary Syntax and Linguistics* and have memorized the required vocabulary and paradigms. As you work on these exercises, it will help most to do as much as you can without looking at the textbook. You might think of the exercises as an informal test of what you have learned after reading and studying the textbook. When you are truly stuck, then go back and look at the textbook for assistance. If you are still unable to answer a question, then look at the answer key provided in this workbook and try to see what you missed or did not understand. But beware—taking shortcuts with the answer key will not help in the long run, so resist the temptation!

We often learn a great deal from our mistakes, so don't stress about trying to get everything correct on the first try. Instead, focus on *learning* from what you missed and *plotting* a course to correct those mistakes. To help in this regard, we have provided opportunities for you to correct and assess your work so that you can then go back and review material that was unclear. After each assigned exercise, there will be a chart that you can use to assist you in identifying what you got wrong and why. If you give your best effort with the exercises and use the textbook and answer key as outlined above, you will learn the most and be encouraged about your progress.

An aside about *writing*: in our digital age, the concept of actually using a pen or pencil to *write* on a piece of *paper* may seem really odd. You may be tempted to type out answers or to use some other electronic medium. Please understand we are great fans of electronic and internet resources, but studies have shown that the physical action of writing is instrumental in facilitating learning and retaining information learned. So we encourage you to *write* (and correct and rewrite) your answers in this workbook.

ABBREVIATIONS

1st	first person
2nd	second person
3rd	third person
acc	accusative case
act	active voice
adj	adjective (adjectival)
adv	adverb(ial)
aor	aorist tense-form
cf.	*confer* (Latin); "compare"
ch./chs.	chapter/chapters
conj	conjunction
dat	dative case
e.g.	*exempli gratia* (Latin); "for example"
fem	feminine
fut	future tense-form
gen	genitive case
GNT	Greek New Testament
i.e.	*id est* (Latin); "that is"
impers	impersonal
impf	imperfect tense-form
impv	imperative mood
ind	indicative mood
inf	infinitive
masc	masculine
mid	middle voice
neut	neuter
nom	nominative case
num	number
pass	passive voice
pf	perfect tense-form
pl	plural
plpf	pluperfect tense-form
prep	preposition
pres	present tense-form
pron	pronoun
ptc	participle
rel	relative
sg	singular
v./vv.	verse/verses

chapter ONE

IMAGE-BEARERS, LANGUAGE, LINGUISTICS, AND GREEK:

From Theological Reflections to Learning the Alphabet

You should complete these assignments after you have studied the material presented in *An Introduction to Biblical Greek Grammar: Elementary Syntax and Linguistics*, chapter 1. You should consider these exercises as a test of what you have learned and memorized. After you have given these exercises your best effort, you should check your work against the answer key.

1. Write out the Greek letters in order three times *from memory*. The ruled lines below will help you to focus on those letters that go above or below the center (dotted) line. It is important that you are able to write Greek letters correctly. Remember a "b" is not the same thing as a β, and a "p" is not the same thing as a ρ!

2. Write the name that corresponds with each Greek letter listed below. For example, the name of the letter ω is "omega."

    a. π ____________

    b. ξ ____________

    c. μ ____________

    d. α ____________

    e. η ____________

3. Write out the lowercase Greek letter that corresponds with the name of each Greek letter listed below.

   a. phi ______________

   b. gamma ______________

   c. beta ______________

   d. zeta ______________

   e. kappa ______________

4. Write out the Greek vowels.

   ____

5. Write out the Greek improper diphthongs.

   ____

6. Write out the three Greek accents using the vowel α, and label each with the name of the accent.

   ____

7. What is the name of the breathing mark over each alpha below?

   a. ἀ: ______________________ breathing mark.
      How does this breathing mark affect pronunciation?

      ____

   b. ἁ: ______________________ breathing mark
      How does this breathing mark affect pronunciation?

      ____

CORRECTION AND ASSESSMENT

Instructions

Once you have completed the assignments to the best of your ability, you may look at the answer key. It is often helpful to assess what you missed and what you can do to learn a particular form or concept more clearly. So on this page, you can assess any mistakes you made and indicate the course of action you can take to address this problem.

question	assessment	course of action
1		

question	assessment	course of action
2		
3		
4		
5		
6		
7		

ANSWER KEY

1. α β γ δ ε ζ η θ ι κ λ μ ν ξ ο π ρ σ/ς τ υ φ χ ψ ω
2. pi, xi, mu, alpha, eta
3. φ, γ, β, ζ, κ
4. α, ε, η, ι, ο, υ, ω
5. ᾳ, ῃ, ῳ
6. ά: acute accent; ᾶ: circumflex accent; ὰ: grave accent
7. a. smooth breathing mark; it does not affect pronunciation
   b. rough breathing mark; there is an "h" sound added before the vowel

READING EXERCISE

Read John 1:1–13. Pronounce each word carefully by paying attention to breaking marks and accents.

1 Ἐν ἀρχῇ ἦν ὁ λόγος, καὶ ὁ λόγος ἦν πρὸς τὸν θεόν, καὶ θεὸς ἦν ὁ λόγος. **2** οὗτος ἦν ἐν ἀρχῇ πρὸς
τὸν θεόν. **3** πάντα δι᾽ αὐτοῦ ἐγένετο, καὶ χωρὶς αὐτοῦ ἐγένετο οὐδὲ ἕν. ὃ γέγονεν **4** ἐν αὐτῷ ζωὴ
ἦν, καὶ ἡ ζωὴ ἦν τὸ φῶς τῶν ἀνθρώπων· **5** καὶ τὸ φῶς ἐν τῇ σκοτίᾳ φαίνει, καὶ ἡ σκοτία αὐτὸ οὐ
κατέλαβεν.

6 Ἐγένετο ἄνθρωπος, ἀπεσταλμένος παρὰ θεοῦ, ὄνομα αὐτῷ Ἰωάννης· **7** οὗτος ἦλθεν εἰς
μαρτυρίαν ἵνα μαρτυρήσῃ περὶ τοῦ φωτός, ἵνα πάντες πιστεύσωσιν δι᾽ αὐτοῦ. **8** οὐκ ἦν ἐκεῖνος τὸ
φῶς, ἀλλ᾽ ἵνα μαρτυρήσῃ περὶ τοῦ φωτός.

9 Ἦν τὸ φῶς τὸ ἀληθινόν, ὃ φωτίζει πάντα ἄνθρωπον, ἐρχόμενον εἰς τὸν κόσμον. **10** ἐν τῷ
κόσμῳ ἦν, καὶ ὁ κόσμος δι᾽ αὐτοῦ ἐγένετο, καὶ ὁ κόσμος αὐτὸν οὐκ ἔγνω. **11** εἰς τὰ ἴδια ἦλθεν, καὶ οἱ
ἴδιοι αὐτὸν οὐ παρέλαβον. **12** ὅσοι δὲ ἔλαβον αὐτόν, ἔδωκεν αὐτοῖς ἐξουσίαν τέκνα θεοῦ γενέσθαι,
τοῖς πιστεύουσιν εἰς τὸ ὄνομα αὐτοῦ, **13** οἳ οὐκ ἐξ αἱμάτων οὐδὲ ἐκ θελήματος σαρκὸς οὐδὲ ἐκ
θελήματος ἀνδρὸς ἀλλ᾽ ἐκ θεοῦ ἐγεννήθησαν.

chapter TWO

THE GREEK VERB FROM CRUISING ALTITUDE: *Fasten Your Seatbelts, Please!*

You should complete these assignments after you have studied the material presented in chapter 2 of the textbook. For this chapter, try to write out your understanding of the concepts presented in your own words. After you have given your best effort, you should check your work against the answer key.

1. Write out a brief definition or description of what each of the following terms means in connection with the Greek verbal system.

   verbal root

   tense stem

   tense-form

   verbal aspect

   verbal person

2. Complete the following chart based on the Greek verb tense-forms. Some of it has already been filled with information that was not explicitly presented in the textbook.

Tense-Form	Aspect	Tense Stem Used to Construct This Tense-Form	Verbal Moods in Which This Tense-Form Occurs	Other Verbal Forms in Which This Tense-Form Occurs
present				
imperfect				
future	debated; "expectation"			
aorist				
perfect	imperfective (probably)			
pluperfect	imperfective (probably)			

3. Briefly indicate the relationship of the subject to a verbal action in the active and passive voices.

4. Briefly describe the middle voice in Greek. How does it compare with the active voice? What does the middle voice *not* primarily indicate?

5. What are two ways in which transitive and intransitive verbs differ from each other?

6. What makes a finite verb "finite"?

___

7. What are the two nonfinite verb forms in Greek? Why are they "nonfinite"?

___

ANSWER KEY

1. verbal root – A verbal root is a verb's most basic morpheme; lexically, it indicates a specific action or state of being; morphologically, it is used to construct a verb's various forms.
   tense stem – A tense stem is the most basic form of a verbal root in a given tense-form.
   tense-form – A tense-form is the resulting form derived from a tense stem. There are six tense-forms in Greek: present and imperfect (both derived from the present stem); future (derived from the future stem); aorist (derived from the aorist stem); and perfect and pluperfect (both derived from the perfect stem).
   verbal aspect – Verbal aspect indicates how a writer or speaker wants an audience to view an action; generally, this is whether the action should be viewed as ongoing (like a video) or simply indicating that the action occurred (like a photo).
   verbal person – Verbal person indicates the relationship between the subject and the verb; in the first person, the subject is the one speaking or writing; in the second person, the subject is the one who is being addressed; in the third person, the subject is the one being written or spoken about.

2.

Tense-Form	Aspect	Tense Stem Used to Construct This Tense-Form	Verbal Moods in Which This Tense-Form Occurs	Other Verbal Forms in Which This Tense-Form Occurs
present	imperfective	present	all	all
imperfect	imperfective	present	indicative only	none
future	debated; "expectation"	future	indicative	limited number of participles and infinitives
aorist	perfective	aorist	all	all
perfect	imperfective	perfect	mainly indicative; limited in imperative and subjunctive	limited number of participles and infinitives
pluperfect	imperfective	perfect	indicative	none

3. In the active voice, the subject acts, whereas in the passive voice, the subject is acted upon.
4. The middle voice also indicates that the subject acts but does so with some emphasis on the subject's participation in that action. It is like the active voice in that it indicates that the subject acts. The middle voice does not primarily indicate a reflexive idea.
5. Transitive verbs can take a direct object, whereas intransitive verbs cannot. Transitive verbs can be made into a passive construction, whereas intransitive verbs cannot.
6. Finite verbs are "finite" because they indicate person and number. In Greek, this is indicated by different inflections, or personal endings. The four finite verb forms in Greek are the indicative, the imperative, the subjunctive, and the optative.
7. The two nonfinite verb forms in Greek are the participle and the infinitive. They are nonfinite verbs because they are not limited by indicating person, although participles can be either singular or plural.

chapter THREE

HOW TO BUILD A VERB:

The Present Active and Middle Indicative

You should complete these assignments after you have studied the material presented in *An Introduction to Biblical Greek Grammar: Elementary Syntax and Linguistics*, chapter 3, and have memorized the required vocabulary and paradigms. You may also want to review the suggestions at the beginning of the workbook.

For each of the following Greek forms, write out the specified components. The first word has been parsed as an example. You should list all possible translations when possible. Any gloss listed in the assigned vocabulary may be used in parsing. Remember to indicate if a component does not apply for the inflected form by writing any of the following: N/A, n/a, or --. Either inflected meaning listed below is acceptable.

inflected form	tense	voice	mood	pers	case	num	gender	lexical form	inflected meaning
γράφομεν	pres	act	ind	1st	n/a	pl	n/a	γράφω	we write we are writing
ἔχετε									
σῴζεσθε									
ἄγουσιν									
ἐσθίει									
ἀκουόμεθα									
αἴρεται									
ἀποστέλλεις									
πείθεσθε									
βαπτίζομαι									
προσεύχεσθε									

(cont.)

inflected form	tense	voice	mood	pers	case	num	gender	lexical form	inflected meaning
θέλεις									
πορεύεται									
εὐαγγελιζόμεθα									
ἐγείρουσιν									
ἀποκρίνῃ									
γίνονται									

CORRECTION AND ASSESSMENT

Instructions

Once you have completed the above assignments to the best of your ability, you may look at the answer key. It is often helpful to assess what you missed and what you can do to learn a particular form or concept more clearly. So on this page, you can assess any mistakes you made and indicate the course of action you can take to address this problem. A sample is provided.

inflected form	assessment	course of action
γράφομεν	mistook 1st pl ending for 2nd pl ending	reviewed primary active personal endings in the present active indicative paradigm of λύω

inflected form	assessment	course of action

ANSWER KEY

Parsing

inflected form	tense	voice	mood	pers	case	num	gender	lexical form	inflected meaning
γράφομεν	pres	act	ind	1st	n/a	pl	n/a	γράφω	we write we are writing
ἔχετε	pres	act	ind	2nd	n/a	pl	n/a	ἔχω	you (pl) have you (pl) are having
σῴζεσθε	pres	mid	ind	2nd	n/a	pl	n/a	σῴζω	you (pl) save for yourselves you (pl) are saving for yourselves
ἄγουσιν	pres	act	ind	3rd	n/a	pl	n/a	ἄγω	they lead they are leading
ἐσθίει	pres	act	ind	3rd	n/a	sg	n/a	ἐσθίω	he/she/it eats he/she/it is eating
ἀκουόμεθα	pres	mid	ind	1st	n/a	pl	n/a	ἀκούω	we hear for ourselves we are hearing for ourselves
αἴρεται	pres	mid	ind	3rd	n/a	sg	n/a	αἴρω	he/she/it takes up for himself/herself/itself he/she/it is taking up for himself/herself/ itself
ἀποστέλλεις	pres	act	ind	2nd	n/a	sg	n/a	ἀποστέλλω	you (sg) send you (sg) are sending
πείθεσθε	pres	mid	ind	2nd	n/a	pl	n/a	πείθω	you (pl) persuade for yourselves you (pl) are persuading for yourselves
βαπτίζομαι	pres	mid	ind	1st	n/a	sg	n/a	βαπτίζω	I baptize myself I am baptizing for myself
προσεύχεσθε	pres	mid	ind	2nd	n/a	pl	n/a	προσεύχομαι	you (pl) pray you (pl) are praying
θέλεις	pres	act	ind	2nd	n/a	sg	n/a	θέλω	you (sg) desire you (sg) are desiring

(cont.)

inflected form	tense	voice	mood	pers	case	num	gender	lexical form	inflected meaning
πορεύεται	pres	mid	ind	3rd	n/a	sg	n/a	πορεύομαι	he/she/it journeys he/she/it is journeying
εὐαγγελιζόμεθα	pres	mid	ind	1st	n/a	pl	n/a	εὐαγγελίζω	we proclaim for ourselves we are proclaiming for ourselves
ἐγείρουσιν	pres	act	ind	3rd	n/a	pl	n/a	ἐγείρω	they raise they are raising
ἀποκρίνῃ	pres	mid	ind	2nd	n/a	sg	n/a	ἀποκρίνομαι	you (sg) answer you (sg) are answering
γίνονται	pres	mid	ind	3rd	n/a	pl	n/a	γίνομαι	they become they are becoming

Additional Notes:

1. With third-person singular verbs, it is always good to list "he/she/it" in the inflected meaning, although in the original context in which the verb occurs, the subject would only be one of these options.
2. You should always indicate "sg" or "pl" for second-person finite verb forms, because the English translation "you" does not make this clear.
3. Present indicative verbs may be rendered with either the simple present or present continuous in English; both options are listed on this answer key for now. In future answer keys, only one option will usually be listed.

chapter **FOUR**

THE GREEK NOUN:

A Case of Form and Function

You should complete these assignments after you have studied the material for chapter 4 in the textbook and memorized the required vocabulary and paradigms. As you work on these assignments, you should avoid using the textbook. Once you have completed these assignments to the best of your ability, you may then look at the answer key.

For each of the following Greek forms, write out the specified components. Be sure to list all possibilities when applicable. Remember to indicate if a component does not apply for the inflected form by writing any of the following: N/A, n/a, or --. The first inflected form has been parsed as an example. Notice that the inflected meanings correspond to each possible parsing. Thus "works" is a possible inflected meaning for ἔργα in both the nominative and accusative cases. Often, however, the inflected meanings will not be the same for words with more than one possible parsing.

inflected form	tense	voice	mood	pers	case	num	gender	lexical form	inflected meaning
ἔργα	n/a	n/a	n/a	n/a	nom acc	pl	neut	ἔργον, -ου, τό	works works
δόξαν									
καρδίας									
κυρίῳ									
ψυχάς									
υἱοῦ									
ἐξουσίαις									
προβάτου									
ὁδόν									
προφήτου									

TRANSLATION

For each of the following sentences, double underline each finite verb. Above each noun, write its case and function. Above each genitival modifier, write GM and draw an arrow from the genitival modifier to its head noun. Then translate the following sentences. The first exercise has been completed as an example. After this chapter, we will no longer mark every noun, but you can continue to do so until these forms and functions are firmly in place.

NOM/ SUBJ (θεὸς) — ACC/ DO (καρδίας)

1. θεὸς δὲ γινώσκει καρδίας.

   But God knows hearts.

2. βλέπω ἀνθρώπους.

3. δέχονται λόγον.

4. ἔρχεται Ἰησοῦς καὶ λαμβάνει ἄρτον.

5. ἐξουσίαν ἔχει υἱὸς ἀνθρώπου.

6. καὶ ἀποστέλλει μαθητάς.

7. ἡμέρᾳ κύριος ἔρχεται.

CORRECTION AND ASSESSMENT

Instructions

Once you have completed the assignments for this chapter to the best of your ability, you may look at the answer key. On this page, you can assess any mistakes you made and indicate the course of action you plan on taking to address the problem.

inflected form or sentence #	assessment	course of action

ANSWER KEY

Parsing

inflected form	tense	voice	mood	pers	case	num	gender	lexical form	inflected meaning
ἔργα	n/a	n/a	n/a	n/a	nom acc	pl	neut	ἔργον, -ου, τό	works works
δόξαν	n/a	n/a	n/a	n/a	acc	sg	fem	δόξα, -ης, ἡ	glory
καρδίας	n/a	n/a	n/a	n/a	gen acc	sg pl	fem	καρδία, -ας, ἡ	of heart hearts
κυρίῳ	n/a	n/a	n/a	n/a	dat	sg	masc	κύριος, -ου, ὁ	to/by/with/in master
ψυχάς	n/a	n/a	n/a	n/a	acc	pl	fem	ψυχή, -ῆς, ἡ	lives
υἱοῦ	n/a	n/a	n/a	n/a	gen	sg	masc	υἱός, -οῦ, ὁ	of son
ἐξουσίαις	n/a	n/a	n/a	n/a	dat	pl	fem	ἐξουσία, -ας, ἡ	to/by/with/in authorities
προβάτου	n/a	n/a	n/a	n/a	gen	sg	neut	πρόβατον, -ου, τό	of sheep
ὁδόν	n/a	n/a	n/a	n/a	acc	sg	fem	ὁδός, -οῦ, ἡ	road
προφήτου	n/a	n/a	n/a	n/a	gen	sg	masc	προφήτης, -ου, ὁ	of prophet

Translation

NOM/ SUBJ — ACC/ DO

1. θεὸς δὲ γινώσκει καρδίας (cf. Luke 16:15)

   But/and God knows hearts.

ACC/ DO

2. βλέπω ἀνθρώπους (cf. Mark 8:24)

   I see men.

ACC/ DO

3. δέχονται λόγον (cf. Luke 8:13)

   They receive [the] word.

NOM/ SUBJ — ACC/ DO

4. ἔρχεται Ἰησοῦς καὶ λαμβάνει ἄρτον (cf. John 21:13)

   Jesus comes and he takes [the] bread.

ACC/ DO — NOM/ SUBJ ← GEN/ GM

5. ἐξουσίαν ἔχει υἱὸς ἀνθρώπου (cf. Matt 9:6)

   [The] son of man has authority.

ACC/ DO

6. καὶ ἀποστέλλει μαθητάς (cf. Mark 14:13)

   And he sends disciples.

DAT/ temp — NOM/ SUBJ

7. ἡμέρᾳ κύριος ἔρχεται (cf. Matt 24:42)

   [The] lord comes on a day.

Additional Notes:

- Each of these sentences has been modified from the GNT; in most instances, the Greek article has been omitted since you have not learned that yet. The addition of the definite article in English (indicated in square brackets) depends on the original context of the sentence in which it occurs in the GNT.
- In sentence 4, notice that the personal pronoun "he" is not used in the translation of the first verb because the subject Ἰησοῦς is explicitly stated. Also notice that the personal pronoun "he" is used with the second verb, although it could also be omitted.
- In sentence 5, notice that the direct object comes before the verb and the subject follows it—this is the flexibility that comes with case endings versus fixed word order.
- In sentence 6, in a different context, the verb ἀποστέλλει could also be translated "she sends." The context in Mark 14:13, however, indicates that Jesus is the one who is sending; hence the translation "he sends."
- Sentence 7, as it stands, could be translated in any of the following ways:

  The lord comes on a day.

  The lord comes on the day.

  A lord comes on a day.

  A lord comes on the day.

  Recall that the dative can indicate a temporal or spatial relationship. In this example, the use of the dative parallels a prepositional phrase, which we will discuss in chapter 6.

chapter FIVE

THE ARTICLE AND THE ADJECTIVE; THE VERB εἰμί

You should complete these assignments after you have studied the material for chapter 5 in the textbook and memorized the required vocabulary and paradigms. As you work on these assignments, you should avoid using the textbook. Once you have completed these assignments to the best of your ability, then check your work with the answer key.

For each of the following Greek forms, write out the specified components. Be sure to list all possibilities when applicable. Remember to indicate if a component does not apply for the inflected form by writing any of the following: N/A, n/a, or --.

inflected form	tense	voice	mood	pers	case	num	gender	lexical form	inflected meaning
καλοῖς									
ἁμαρτάνει									
πιστήν									
δικαίων									
εἰσί									
ἁμαρτωλοί									
ἁγίῳ									
σημεῖα									
νεκρούς									
φόβου									

TRANSLATION

- For each of the following sentences, double underline each finite verb.
- Above each genitival modifier, write GM and draw an arrow from the genitival modifier to its head noun.
- Single underline each adjective.
- Above each adjective write its function: attributive (ATTR), substantival (SUB), or predicate (PRED).
- Translate the following sentences.

Pop-Up Lexicon

διαλογισμός, οῦ, ὁ thought, opinion

The first exercise has been completed as an example.

SUB
GM

1. κύριος γινώσκει τοὺς διαλογισμοὺς τῶν σοφῶν (1 Cor 3:20)

The Lord knows the thoughts of the wise ones.

2. τυφλοὶ ἀναβλέπουσιν καὶ κωφοὶ ἀκούουσιν.

3. ὁ θεός ἐγείρει τοὺς νεκρούς.

4. ἡ τελεία ἀγάπη ἔξω βάλλει τὸν φόβον.

5. καὶ τότε φαίνεται τὸ σημεῖον τοῦ υἱοῦ τοῦ ἀνθρώπου.

6. ὁ θεὸς ἀγάπη ἐστίν.

7. κύριος κυρίων ἐστίν.

8. ἄνθρωποι ἐστε ἀγάπης.

CORRECTION AND ASSESSMENT

Instructions

Once you have completed the parsing and translation exercises to the best of your ability, look at the answer key. On this page, you will find space to assess any mistakes you made and to indicate the course of action you took to address the problem.

inflected form or sentence #	assessment	course of action

ANSWER KEY

Parsing

inflected form	tense	voice	mood	pers	case	num	gender	lexical form	inflected meaning
καλοῖς	n/a	n/a	n/a	n/a	dat	pl	masc neut	καλός, -ή, -όν	to/by/with/in good [ones] to/by/with/in good [ones]
ἁμαρτάνει	pres	act	ind	3rd	n/a	sg	n/a	ἁμαρτάνω	he/she/it sins he/she/it is sinning
πιστήν	n/a	n/a	n/a	n/a	acc	sg	fem	πιστός, -ή, -όν	faithful [ones]
δικαίων	n/a	n/a	n/a	n/a	gen	pl	masc fem neut	δίκαιος, -α, -ον	of righteous [ones] of righteous [ones] of righteous [ones]
εἰσί	pres	n/a	ind	3rd	n/a	pl	n/a	εἰμί	they are
ἁμαρτωλοί	n/a	n/a	n/a	n/a	nom	pl	masc fem	ἁμαρτωλός, -όν	sinful [ones]
ἁγίῳ	n/a	n/a	n/a	n/a	dat	sg	masc neut	ἅγιος, -α, -ον	to [a] holy [one] to [a] holy [one]
σημεῖα	n/a	n/a	n/a	n/a	nom acc	pl	neut	σημεῖον, -ου, τό	signs signs
νεκρούς	n/a	n/a	n/a	n/a	acc	pl	masc	νεκρός, -ά, -όν	dead [ones]
φόβου	n/a	n/a	n/a	n/a	gen	sg	masc	φόβος, -ου, ὁ	of fear

Additional Notes:

- For the inflected meaning, a substantival function of the adjective is assumed and is indicated by [one] or [ones] in these exercises. In the context of actual sentences from the GNT, an adjective may be functioning substantivally, attributively, or as a predicate. If the adjective is substantival, the assumed entity is often clear from the context and may be added to the translation. For example, if καλοῖς were referring to people, then the translation could reflect this with "to/by/with/in good people," whereas if it were referring to inanimate objects, then the translation could reflect this with "to/by/with/in good things."
- The context will usually make clear if a substantive (including a substantival adjective) is definite or not. We have added an indefinite article to the translation of ἁγίῳ, but in an actual GNT sentence, it could also be "to the holy one."

Translation

SUB
GM

1. κύριος <u>γινώσκει</u> τοὺς διαλογισμοὺς τῶν <u>σοφῶν</u> (1 Cor 3:20)

   The Lord knows the thoughts of the wise ones.

SUB SUB

2. τυφλοὶ ἀναβλέπουσιν καὶ κωφοὶ ἀκούουσιν (cf. Matt 11:5)

Blind ones receive sight and deaf ones hear.

SUB

3. ὁ θεός ἐγείρει τοὺς νεκρούς (cf. John 5:21)

God raises the dead.

ATTR →

4. ἡ τελεία ἀγάπη ἔξω βάλλει τὸν φόβον (1 John 4:18)

Perfect love casts out fear.

← GM ← GM

5. καὶ τότε φαίνεται τὸ σημεῖον τοῦ υἱοῦ τοῦ ἀνθρώπου (cf. Matt 24:30)

And then the sign of the son of man appears.

6. ὁ θεὸς ἀγάπη ἐστίν (1 John 4:8)

God is love.

← GM

7. κύριος κυρίων ἐστίν (Rev 17:14)

He is the Lord of lords.

← GM

8. ἄνθρωποι ἐστε ἀγάπης

You are people of love.

Additional Notes:

- Note the presence of the article in the English translation for sentence 1. The larger context makes it clear that κύριος is definite in 1 Corinthians 3:20. The two substantival adjectives in sentence 2 could be translated with or without the definite article in English.
- In 1 Corinthians 3:20, Matthew 11:5, and John 5:21, the overall context of each sentence makes it clear that the adjective is functioning substantivally. With each of these substantival adjectives, notice that there is no substantive in close proximity to the adjective with the same case, number, and gender. So the adjective could not be functioning attributively. Additionally, it is not always necessary to add "ones" with substantival adjectives. For example, 1 Corinthians 3:20 could be translated, "The Lord knows the thoughts of the wise," and Matthew 11:5 could be translated, "The blind receive sight and the deaf hear."
- Sentence 4 is a good example of the use of the article in Greek. Abstract nouns, such as love, are often articular in Greek but are not translated with an article in English (e.g., "love," not "the love"). Although

God is not an abstract noun, notice that θεός is articular in Greek, but is not translated with the definite article in English (e.g., "God," not "the God").

- In sentence 7, the subject "he" is understood from the larger context—besides, "the Lord is of lords" doesn't make any sense! If you missed this one, don't worry. It's a bit challenging.

chapter SIX

PREPOSITIONS, PERSONAL PRONOUNS, AND BASIC CONJUNCTIONS

You should complete these assignments after you have studied the material for chapter 6 in the textbook and memorized the required vocabulary and paradigms. Once you have completed these assignments to the best of your ability, you should check your work with the answer key.

For each of the following Greek forms, write out the specified components. Be sure to list all possibilities when applicable. Remember to indicate if a component does not apply for the inflected form by writing any of the following: N/A, n/a, or --.

TRANSLATION

inflected form	tense	voice	mood	pers	case	num	gender	lexical form	inflected meaning
ἡμῶν									
ὥρας									
προσέρχονται									
φωναῖς									
πρώτη									
αὐτῇ									
ὑμῖν									
κόσμον									
μου									
αὐτό									

- For each of the following sentences, double underline each finite verb.
- Above each genitival modifier, write GM and draw an arrow from the genitival modifier to its head noun.
- Put brackets around every [prepositional phrase].
- Single underline each adjective and pronoun.
- Above each adjective write its function: attributive (ATTR), substantival (SUB), or predicate (PRED).
- Highlight each subordinating conjunction.
- Put a parenthesis around each (subordinate clause).
- Translate the following sentences.

1. ἀλλὰ ὑμεῖς οὐ πιστεύετε, ὅτι οὐκ ἐστὲ ἐκ τῶν προβάτων μου.

____

2. δόξαν ἀπ᾽ ἀνθρώπων οὐ λαμβάνω.

____

3. προσεύχομαι τῷ θεῷ.

____

4. ὁ δὲ Ἰησοῦς πορεύεται σὺν αὐτοῖς.

____

5. καὶ προσέρχονται αὐτῷ τυφλοὶ ἐν τῇ ὁδῷ, καὶ θεράπευει αὐτούς.

____

6. ἐγὼ δὲ ὅτι τὴν ἀλήθειαν λέγω, οὐ πιστεύετέ μοι.

____

7. ἐκλέγεται ἡμᾶς ἐν αὐτῷ πρὸ καταβολῆς κόσμου.

____

CORRECTION AND ASSESSMENT

Instructions

Once you have completed the parsing and translation exercises to the best of your ability, look at the answer key. On this page, you will find spaces to assess any mistakes you made and to indicate the course of action you took to address the problem.

inflected form or sentence #	assessment	course of action

ANSWER KEY

Parsing

inflected form	tense	voice	mood	pers	case	num	gender	lexical form	inflected meaning
ἡμῶν	n/a	n/a	n/a	n/a	gen	pl	n/a	ἐγώ	our
ὥρας	n/a	n/a	n/a	n/a	gen acc	sg pl	fem	ὥρα, -ας, ἡ	of (an) hour hours
προσέρχονται	pres	mid	ind	3rd	n/a	pl	n/a	προσέρχομαι	they go toward they are going toward
φωναῖς	n/a	n/a	n/a	n/a	dat	pl	fem	φωνή, -ῆς, ἡ	to/by/with/in (a) voice
πρώτη	n/a	n/a	n/a	n/a	nom	sg	fem	πρῶτος, -η, -ον	first [one]
αὐτῇ	n/a	n/a	n/a	n/a	dat	sg	fem	αὐτός, αὐτή, αὐτό	to/by/with/in her
ὑμῖν	n/a	n/a	n/a	n/a	dat	pl	n/a	σύ	to/by/with/in you (pl)
κόσμον	n/a	n/a	n/a	n/a	acc	sg	masc	κόσμος, -ου, ὁ	(a) world
μου	n/a	n/a	n/a	n/a	gen	sg	n/a	ἐγώ	my
αὐτό	n/a	n/a	n/a	n/a	nom acc	sg	neut	αὐτός, αὐτή, αὐτό	it it

Translation

ATTR

1. ἀλλὰ ὑμεῖς οὐ πιστεύετε, (ὅτι οὐκ ἐστὲ [ἐκ τῶν προβάτων μου]). (cf. John 10:26)

   But you yourselves do not believe, because you are not from my sheep.

2. δόξαν [ἀπ᾽ ἀνθρώπων] οὐ λαμβάνω (cf. John 5:41)

   I do not receive glory from humanity.

3. προσεύχομαι τῷ θεῷ.

   I pray to God.

4. ὁ δὲ Ἰησοῦς πορεύεται [σὺν αὐτοῖς]. (cf. Luke 7:6)

   And/but Jesus goes with them.

SUB

5. καὶ προσέρχονται αὐτῷ τυφλοὶ [ἐν τῇ ὁδῷ], καὶ θεράπευει αὐτούς. (cf. Matt 21:14)

   And the blind go to him on the road, and he heals them.

6. ἐγὼ δὲ (ὅτι τὴν ἀλήθειαν λέγω), οὐ πιστεύετέ μοι. (John 8:45)

   And/but because I myself am telling the truth, you do not believe me.

GM

7. ἐκλέγεται ἡμᾶς [ἐν αὐτῷ] [πρὸ καταβολῆς κόσμου] (cf. Eph 1:4)

   He chooses us in him before the foundation of the world.

Additional Notes:

- Notice the emphatic use of the personal pronoun in sentence 1. Recall that a finite verb does not need a pronoun to indicate its subject, so any occurrence of a personal pronoun in the nominative case indicates emphasis.
- The text in sentence 5 is adapted from Matthew 21:14, which occurs in a narrative section of Matthew, so this verse could also be translated with English past-tense verbs; for example: "And the blind were going to him on the road, and he healed them." This sentence was modified because the original text has different tense-forms that you haven't learned yet. Also if you translated τυφλοί as "blind people" without an article, that is also a correct translation.
- Notice the emphatic use of the personal pronoun in sentence 6. In this same verse, μοι is called an **enclitic** because it has "thrown" its accent back onto πιστεύετε, which is why the verb has two accents. The verb πιστεύω can take a direct object in the dative case, as noted in the vocabulary.

chapter **SEVEN**

THE IMPERFECT ACTIVE AND MIDDLE INDICATIVE; MORE ON PREPOSITIONS

You should complete these assignments after you have studied the material for chapter 7 in the textbook and memorized the required vocabulary and paradigms. Once you have completed these assignments to the best of your ability, you should check your answers with the answer key.

For each of the following Greek forms, write out the specified components. Be sure to list all possibilities when applicable. Remember to indicate if a component does not apply for the inflected form by writing any of the following: N/A, n/a, or --.

inflected form	tense	voice	mood	pers	case	num	gender	lexical form	inflected meaning
ὑπέστρεφον									
εὕρισκες									
ἐμῇ									
ἔμενεν									
ἐπορευόμην									
εὐηγγελίζοντο									
ἐγειρόμεθα									
ἐκράζεσθε									
ἐγίνετο									
ἐλαμβάνου									

TRANSLATION

- For each of the following sentences, double underline each finite verb.
- Above each genitival modifier, write GM and draw an arrow from the genitival modifier to its head noun.
- Put brackets around every [prepositional phrase].
- Single underline each adjective and pronoun.
- Above each adjective write its function: attributive (ATTR), substantival (SUB), or predicate (PRED).
- Highlight each subordinating conjunction.
- Put a parenthesis around each (subordinate clause).
- Translate the following sentences.

1. ὑπέστρεφον εἰς Ἱεροσόλυμα.

____

2. αὐτοὶ νόμον ἐφυλάσσοντο.

____

3. ἤκουον δὲ τοὺς λογούς αὐτῶν οἱ Φαρισαῖοι.

____

4. καὶ οἱ μαθηταί ἤρχοντο, καὶ ἐδίδασκεν αὐτούς.

____

5. Ἰησοῦς αὐτὸς οὐκ ἐβάπτιζεν ἀλλ' οἱ μαθηταὶ αὐτοῦ.

____

6. Μωϋσῆς ἐθαύμαζεν τὸ σημεῖον.

____

7. αὐτὸς δὲ Ἰησοῦς οὐκ ἐπίστευεν αὐτὸν αὐτοῖς.

____

CORRECTION AND ASSESSMENT

Instructions

Once you have completed the parsing and translation exercises to the best of your ability, you may then look at the answer key. On this page, you will find spaces to assess any mistakes you made and to indicate the course of action you took to address the problem.

inflected form or sentence #	assessment	course of action

ANSWER KEY

Parsing

inflected form	tense	voice	mood	pers	case	num	gender	lexical form	inflected meaning
ὑπέστρεφον	impf	act	ind	1st 3rd	n/a	sg pl	n/a	ὑποστρέφω	I was returning they were returning
εὕρισκες	impf	act	ind	2nd	n/a	sg	n/a	εὑρίσκω	you (sg) were finding
ἐμῇ	n/a	n/a	n/a	n/a	dat	sg	fem	ἐμός, -η, -ον	to/by/with/in my [one]
ἔμενεν	impf	act	ind	3rd	n/a	sg	n/a	μένω	he/she/it was remaining
ἐπορευόμην	impf	mid	ind	1st	n/a	sg	n/a	πορεύομαι	I was going
εὐηγγελίζοντο	impf	mid	ind	3rd	n/a	pl	n/a	εὐαγγελίζω	they were preaching good news for themselves
ἐγειρόμεθα	pres	mid	ind	1st	n/a	pl	n/a	ἐγείρω	We raise for ourselves
ἐκράζεσθε	impf	mid	ind	2nd	n/a	pl	n/a	κράζω	you (pl) were crying out for yourselves
ἐγίνετο	impf	mid	ind	3rd	n/a	sg	n/a	γίνομαι	he/she/it was becoming
ἐλαμβάνου	impf	mid	ind	2nd	n/a	sg	n/a	λαμβάνω	you (sg) were taking for yourself

Translation

1. ὑπέστρεφον [εἰς Ἱεροσόλυμα] (Acts 8:25)

   They were returning to Jerusalem.

2. αὐτοὶ νόμον ἐφυλάσσοντο (cf. Gal 6:13)

   They themselves were keeping the law.

3. ἤκουον δὲ τοὺς λογούς αὐτῶν οἱ Φαρισαῖοι (cf. Luke 16:14) [GM]

   And/but the Pharisees were hearing their words.

4. καὶ οἱ μαθηταί ἤρχοντο, καὶ ἐδίδασκεν αὐτούς (cf. Mark 2:13)

   And the disciples were coming, and he began to teach them.

5. Ἰησοῦς αὐτὸς οὐκ ἐβάπτιζεν ἀλλ᾽ οἱ μαθηταὶ αὐτοῦ (John 4:2) [GM]

   Jesus himself was not baptizing, but his disciples [were baptizing].

6. Μωϋσῆς ἐθαύμαζεν τὸ σημεῖον (cf. Acts 7:31)

   Moses was marveling at the miracle.

7. αὐτὸς δὲ Ἰησοῦς οὐκ ἐπίστευεν αὐτὸν αὐτοῖς (John 2:24)

   But Jesus himself was not entrusting himself to them.

Additional Notes:

- Notice the use of the imperfect in sentence 4. The translation "he began to teach" indicates an ingressive nuance from the imperfect. You may have translated this "he was teaching them," which is also an acceptable translation.
- Notice the use of ellipsis in sentence 5—the finite verb is not repeated in the second clause, but it is understood. So you could also translate this verse as follows: "Jesus himself was not baptizing, but his disciples were baptizing" (as indicated in the square brackets), or even "Jesus himself was not baptizing, but his disciples were."

chapter EIGHT

TEXT FOR INTEGRATION

You can make a copy of this text to accompany your work on the integration exercises for chapter 8 in the textbook.

1. καὶ ἐν ταῖς πρώταις ἡμέραις οἱ μαθηταὶ εὐηγγέλιζον καὶ ἐκήρυσσον τὴν βασιλείαν

2. τοῦ θεοῦ ταὶς ἐκκλησίαις. Αὐτὸς δὲ Ἰησοῦς προσέρχεται αὐταῖς καὶ ἐδίδασκεν αὐτάς

3. ἐν παραβολαῖς. Ἐν αὐτῷ ζωὴ ἐστίν, καὶ ἡ ζωὴ ἐστίν ἡ ἐπαγγελία ἡ ἀπὸ τῶν οὐρανῶν.

4. τὰ πρῶτα σημεῖα τοῦ θεοῦ αὐτοὶ πιστεύουσιν·

5. αὐτοὶ γὰρ γινώσκομεν ὅτι ὁ Ἰησοῦς ἐστίν ὁ κύριος τοῦ κόσμου.

6. καὶ ἡμεῖς μένομεν ἐν σοι ὅτι σὺ εἶ ὁ ἅγιος τοῦ θεοῦ.

7. καὶ δοξάζομεν τὸν υἱὸν τοῦ θεοῦ.

chapter NINE

RELATIVES, DEMONSTRATIVES, AND MORE PREPOSITIONS

You should complete these assignments after you have studied the material for chapter 9 in the textbook and memorized the required vocabulary and paradigms. Once you have completed these assignments to the best of your ability, you should check your work with the answer key.

For each of the following Greek forms, write out the specified components. Be sure to list all possibilities when applicable. Remember to indicate if a component does not apply for the inflected form by writing any of the following: N/A, n/a, or --.

inflected form	tense	voice	mood	pers	case	num	gender	lexical form	inflected meaning
ἐκεῖνο									
τούτων									
ἐκείνου									
ταύτῃ									
αὐτῇ									
ἐκείνοις									
αὗται									
αὐταῖς									
αὐτό									
ταῦτα									

TRANSLATION

- For each of the following sentences, double underline each finite verb.
- Above each genitival modifier, write GM and draw an arrow from the genitival modifier to its head noun.
- Put brackets around every [prepositional phrase].
- Single underline each adjective and each pronoun other than a relative pronoun.
- Above each adjective write its function: attributive (ATTR), substantival (SUB), or predicate (PRED).
- Highlight each subordinating conjunction and relative pronoun.
- Put a parenthesis around each (subordinate clause) or (relative clause).
- If applicable, draw an arrow from each relative pronoun to its antecedent.
- Translate the following sentences.

Pop-Up Lexicon

αἰώνιος, -ον   eternal

1. ἀγαπητοί, οὐκ ἐντολὴν καινὴν γράφω ὑμῖν ἀλλ᾽ ἐντολὴν παλαιὰν ἣν εἴχετε ἀπὸ πρώτης ἡμέρας.

2. καὶ ἐγώ ἃ ἤκουον ἀπ᾽ αὐτοῦ ταῦτα λέγω εἰς τὸν κόσμον.

3. καὶ αὕτη ἐστὶν ἡ ἐπαγγελία ἣν αὐτὸς ἔλεγεν ἡμῖν—τὴν ζωὴν τὴν αἰώνιον.

4. ἄξιοί ἐστε τῆς βασιλείας τοῦ θεοῦ, ὑπὲρ ἧς καὶ διώκεσθε.

5. καὶ ἐγίνετο ἐν ἐκείναις ταῖς ἡμέραις ἔρχεται Ἰησοῦς ἀπὸ Ναζαρὲτ[1] τῆς Γαλιλαίας.

6. καὶ εὐθέως ἐν ταῖς ἐκκλησίαις ἐκήρυσσεν τὸν Ἰησοῦν ὅτι οὗτός ἐστιν ὁ υἱὸς τοῦ θεοῦ.

1. This word will not be assigned in the vocabulary, but we're guessing that you can figure it out. If not, you can find it in the lexicon.

7. ἰδοὺ ἀποστέλλω τὸν ἄγγελόν μου πρὸ σου, ὃς κατασκευάζει τὴν ὁδόν σου.

____

CORRECTION AND ASSESSMENT

Instructions

Once you have completed the above parsing and translation exercises to the best of your ability, you may then look at the answer key. On this page, you will find spaces to assess any mistakes you made and to indicate the course of action you took to address the problem.

inflected form or sentence #	assessment	course of action

ANSWER KEY

Parsing

inflected form	tense	voice	mood	pers	case	num	gender	lexical form	inflected meaning
ἐκεῖνο	n/a	n/a	n/a	n/a	nom acc	sg	neut	ἐκεῖνος, -η, -ο	that [one]
τούτων	n/a	n/a	n/a	n/a	gen	pl	masc fem neut	οὗτος, αὕτη, τοῦτο	of these [ones]
ἐκείνου	n/a	n/a	n/a	n/a	gen	sg	masc neut	ἐκεῖνος, -η, -ο	of that [one]

inflected form	tense	voice	mood	pers	case	num	gender	lexical form	inflected meaning
ταύτῃ	n/a	n/a	n/a	n/a	dat	sg	fem	οὗτος, αὕτη, τοῦτο	to/by/with/in this [one]
αὐτῇ	n/a	n/a	n/a	n/a	dat	sg	fem	αὐτός, αὐτή, αὐτό	to/by/with/in her
ἐκείνοις	n/a	n/a	n/a	n/a	dat	pl	masc neut	ἐκεῖνος, -η, -ο	to/by/with/in those [ones]
αὗται	n/a	n/a	n/a	n/a	nom	pl	fem	οὗτος, αὕτη, τοῦτο	these [ones]
αὐταῖς	n/a	n/a	n/a	n/a	dat	pl	fem	αὐτός, αὐτή, αὐτό	to/by/with/in them
αὐτό	n/a	n/a	n/a	n/a	nom acc	sg	neut	αὐτός, αὐτή, αὐτό	it
ταῦτα	n/a	n/a	n/a	n/a	nom acc	pl	neut	οὗτος, αὕτη, τοῦτο	these [ones]

Translation

SUB ATTR ATTR

1. ἀγαπητοί, οὐκ ἐντολὴν καινὴν γράφω ὑμῖν ἀλλ' ἐντολὴν παλαιὰν (ἣν εἴχετε [ἀπὸ πρώτης ἡμέρας]) (cf. 1 John 2:7)

   Beloved, I am not writing a new commandment to you but an old commandment that you have from the first day.

2. καὶ ἐγώ (ἃ ἤκουον [ἀπ' αὐτοῦ]) ταῦτα λέγω [εἰς τὸν κόσμον] (cf. John 8:26)

   And I myself say these things, which I was hearing from him, in the world.

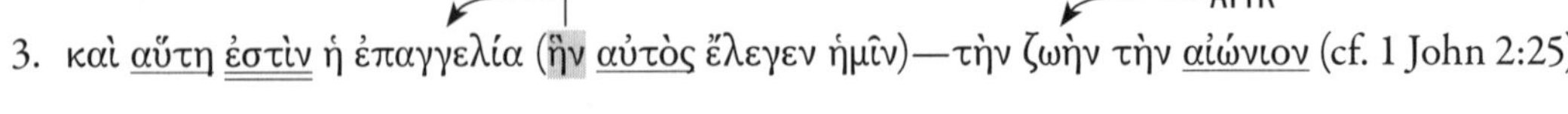

3. καὶ αὕτη ἐστὶν ἡ ἐπαγγελία (ἣν αὐτὸς ἔλεγεν ἡμῖν)—τὴν ζωὴν τὴν αἰώνιον (cf. 1 John 2:25)

   And this is the promise that he himself was saying to us—eternal life.

SUB GM

4. ἄξιοί ἐστε τῆς βασιλείας τοῦ θεοῦ, ([ὑπὲρ ἧς] καὶ διώκεσθε) (cf. 2 Thess 1:5)

   You are worthy of the kingdom of God, for which you are also being persecuted.

ATTR GM

5. καὶ ἐγίνετο [ἐν ἐκείναις ταῖς ἡμέραις] ἔρχεται Ἰησοῦς [ἀπὸ Ναζαρὲτ τῆς Γαλιλαίας] (cf. Mark 1:9)

   And it was happening in those days, Jesus comes from Nazareth of Galilee.

GM

6. καὶ εὐθέως [ἐν ταῖς ἐκκλησίαις] ἐκήρυσσεν τὸν Ἰησοῦν (ὅτι οὗτός ἐστιν ὁ υἱὸς τοῦ θεοῦ) (cf. Acts 9:20)

   And immediately he began to preach Jesus in the assemblies, "This one is the son of God."

GM GM

7. ἰδοὺ ἀποστέλλω τὸν ἄγγελόν μου [πρὸ σου], (ὃς κατασκευάζει τὴν ὁδόν σου) (cf. Mark 1:2)

See! I am sending my messenger before you, who is preparing your way.

Additional Notes:

- Notice the use of the vocative in sentence 1. The form of the vocative plural is the same as the form of the nominative plural. The context makes it clear that the vocative is intended because John is directly addressing the recipients of this epistle.
- The fact that two anarthrous attributive adjectives occur in sentence 1 is a bit unusual, but it is clear from the context how each of these adjectives is functioning.
- The final verb in sentence 1 is from ἔχω; the imperfect form of this verb is a bit irregular. You might have expected the augment to have caused the initial epsilon of the present stem to have lengthened to an eta; instead the diphthong ει occurs because of a "phantom" letter that no longer occurs in this stem but which makes its presence known in this unusual form of the augment. If you are curious, you can read about this in William D. Mounce, *The Morphology of Biblical Greek* (Grand Rapids: Zondervan, 1994), 260n10.
- Notice that the article does not occur in the prepositional phrase in sentence 1, which is common. Even so, since there is only one "first day," the noun is definite, and the article is required in English.
- In sentence 2, the referent for the relative pronoun follows it, so ταῦτα is technically a postcedent.
- In sentence 3, notice that English does not use the definite article with "eternal life" even though the construction is articular in Greek.
- The relative pronoun in sentence 3 is a good example of how the case of the antecedent and the case of the relative pronoun are determined by their function in their respective clauses. The relative clause ἥν is accusative because it is the direct object of the verb ἔλεγεν in the relative clause; its antecedent, ἐπαγγελία, is nominative because it is a predicate nominative.
- In sentence 4, the adjective ἄξιοι requires that the word it is describing be in the genitive case. So although τῆς βασιλείας is in the genitive case, it is not functioning as a genitival modifier. Instead, the genitive case is required because of ἄξιοι.
- The verb γίνομαι is a bit idiomatic in narratives (an example of which occurs in the excerpt from Mark 1:9 in sentence 5). We will discuss this more fully in chapter 14, but for now, you might want to compare the way that this is rendered in various English translations.
- In sentence 6, notice that ὅτι functions in Greek similar to the way that quotation marks function in English—to introduce a direct citation.
- The relative pronoun in sentence 7 is another good example of how the case of the antecedent and the case of the relative pronoun are determined by their function in their respective clauses. The relative pronoun ὅς is nominative because it is the subject of the verb κατασκευάζει in the relative clause; its antecedent, ἄγγελον, is accusative because it is the direct object of ἀποστέλλω.

chapter TEN

ROOTS, STEMS, AND PRINCIPAL PARTS; THE AORIST ACTIVE AND MIDDLE INDICATIVE

You should complete these assignments after you have studied the material for chapter 10 in the textbook and memorized the required vocabulary, paradigms, and principal parts. *Beginning with this chapter*, you are being assigned principal parts to memorize. This means that there are verbs that you have memorized as vocabulary words but whose principal parts you have not yet memorized. So when you encounter a verb form in the exercises whose lexical form you do not immediately recognize, try to think through the principal parts that you know to see if you can identify the verb. If you still do not recognize the verb, then you may consult the "Principal Parts Chart" (in appendix 14 of the textbook). Once you have completed these exercises to the best of your ability, check your work with the answer key.

For each of the following Greek forms, write out the specified components. Be sure to list all possibilities when applicable. Remember to indicate if a component does not apply for the inflected form by writing any of the following: N/A, n/a, or --.

inflected form	tense	voice	mood	pers	case	num	gender	lexical form	inflected meaning
ἐπέμψαμεν									
ἤκουσεν									
ἔμεινα									
ἐκαθάρισεν									
ἐλάμβανον									
ἔβλεψα									
ἤγειρεν									
ἐγενόμεθα									
ἤλθομεν									
ἐκήρυξαν									

TRANSLATION

- For each of the following sentences, double underline each finite verb.
- Above each genitival modifier, write GM and draw an arrow from the genitival modifier to its head noun.
- Put brackets around every [prepositional phrase].
- Single underline each adjective and each pronoun other than a relative pronoun.
- Above each adjective write its function: attributive (ATTR), substantival (SUB), or predicate (PRED).
- Highlight each subordinating conjunction and relative pronoun.
- Put a parenthesis around each (subordinate clause) or (relative clause).
- If applicable, draw an arrow from each relative pronoun to its antecedent.
- Translate the following sentences.

Pop-Up Lexicon

ἁμαρτία, -ας, ἡ	sin
χρόνος, -ου, ὁ	time, period of time

1. ἔλαβεν δὲ φόβος αὐτούς καὶ ἐδόξαζον τὸν θεόν.

____

2. καὶ ἐγένετο μετὰ ἡμέρας τρεῖς εὗρον αὐτὸν ἐν τῷ ἱερῷ.

____

3. ὅτε δὲ ἦλθεν ὁ χρόνος, ἀπέστειλεν ὁ θεὸς τὸν υἱὸν αὐτοῦ.

____

4. καὶ ἐξέβαλον αὐτὸν ἔξω.

____

5. ἦλθεν γὰρ Ἰωάννης πρὸς ὑμᾶς ἐν ὁδῷ δικαιοσύνης, καὶ οὐκ ἐπιστεύσατε αὐτῷ, οἱ δὲ τελῶναι ἐπίστευσαν αὐτῷ.

____

____

6. εἰς τὰ ἴδια ἦλθεν, καὶ οἱ ἴδιοι αὐτὸν οὐ παρέλαβον.

7. εἶπεν αὐτοῖς ὁ Ἰησοῦς, εἰ τυφλοὶ ἦτε, οὐκ ἂν εἴχετε ἁμαρτίαν· νῦν δὲ λέγετε ὅτι βλέπομεν, ἡ ἁμαρτία ὑμῶν μένει.

CORRECTION AND ASSESSMENT

Instructions

Once you have completed the parsing and translation exercises to the best of your ability, you may then look at the answer key. On this page, you will find spaces to assess any mistakes you made and to indicate the course of action you took to address the problem.

inflected form or sentence #	assessment	course of action

ANSWER KEY

Parsing

inflected form	tense	voice	mood	pers	case	num	gender	lexical form	inflected meaning
ἐπέμψαμεν	aor (1st)	act	ind	1st	n/a	pl	n/a	πέμπω	we sent
ἤκουσεν	aor (1st)	act	ind	3rd	n/a	sg	n/a	ἀκούω	he/she/it heard
ἔμεινα	aor (liquid)	act	ind	1st	n/a	sg	n/a	μένω	I remained
ἐκαθάρισεν	aor (1st)	act	ind	3rd	n/a	sg	n/a	καθαρίζω	he/she/it cleansed
ἐλάμβανον	impf	act	ind	1st 3rd	n/a	sg pl	n/a	λαμβάνω	I was taking they were taking
ἔβλεψα	aor (1st)	act	ind	1st	n/a	sg	n/a	βλέπω	I saw
ἤγειρεν	aor (liquid)	act	ind	3rd	n/a	sg	n/a	ἐγείρω	he/she/it raised
ἐγενόμεθα	aor (2nd)	mid	ind	1st	n/a	pl	n/a	γίνομαι	we became
ἤλθομεν	aor (2nd)	act	ind	1st	n/a	pl	n/a	ἔρχομαι	we came/went
ἐκήρυξαν	aor (1st)	act	ind	3rd	n/a	pl	n/a	κηρύσσω	they preached

Additional Notes:

- We have included first-, second-, and liquid-aorist labeling in the answer key for your reference in this chapter only. You do not need to list these in your parsing, but it is always helpful to know whether a verb is first or second aorist, or if it is a liquid stem.
- Always keep in mind that an English simple past is the "default" inflected meaning for the aorist, but the larger context in which a verb occurs determines the best way to render the verb in English.

Translation

1. ἔλαβεν δὲ φόβος αὐτούς καὶ ἐδόξαζον τὸν θεόν (cf. Luke 7:16)

   And fear took them, and they were glorifying God.

   ← ATTR

2. καὶ ἐγένετο [μετὰ ἡμέρας τρεῖς] εὗρον αὐτὸν [ἐν τῷ ἱερῷ] (Luke 2:46)

   ~~And it happened that after three days I found him in the temple.~~

   And it happened that after three days they found him in the temple.

GM

3. (ὅτε δὲ ἦλθεν ὁ χρόνος), ἀπέστειλεν ὁ θεὸς τὸν υἱὸν αὐτοῦ (cf. Gal 4:4)

And when the time came, God sent his Son.

4. καὶ ἐξέβαλον αὐτὸν ἔξω (John 9:34)

~~And I threw him outside.~~

And they threw him outside.

GM

5. ἦλθεν γὰρ Ἰωάννης [πρὸς ὑμᾶς] [ἐν ὁδῷ δικαιοσύνης], καὶ οὐκ ἐπιστεύσατε αὐτῷ, οἱ δὲ τελῶναι . . . ἐπίστευσαν αὐτῷ (Matt 21:32)

For John came to you in the way of righteousness, and you did not believe him, but tax collectors . . . believed him.

SUB SUB

6. [εἰς τὰ ἴδια] ἦλθεν, καὶ οἱ ἴδιοι αὐτὸν οὐ παρέλαβον (John 1:11)

He came to his own, and his own [people] did not receive him.

PRED

7. εἶπεν αὐτοῖς ὁ Ἰησοῦς, (εἰ τυφλοὶ ἦτε), οὐκ ἂν εἴχετε ἁμαρτίαν· νῦν δὲ λέγετε (ὅτι βλέπομεν),

GM

ἡ ἁμαρτία ὑμῶν μένει (John 9:41)

Jesus said to them, "If you were blind, you would not have sin; but now you say, 'We are seeing,' your sin remains."

Additional Notes:

- Notice the shift from the aorist to the imperfect in sentence 1—this is not unusual.
- The lexicon lists "I take, I receive, I obtain" as possible glosses for λαμβάνω, but you'll notice a wide range of translations in English versions for this verb. Now might be a good time to compare multiple versions.
- Although you may have translated sentence 2 (Luke 2:46) as "and it happened after three days I found him in the temple," the larger context of Luke 2 makes it clear that the verb εὗρον is third-person plural, which is why this option has been crossed out.
- In sentence 4, the larger context of John 9 makes it clear that the verb ἐξέβαλον is third-person plural, so the first-person option has been crossed out.
- In sentence 5, the verb ἦλθεν could be translated either "[John] came" or "[John] went"; in this context "came" makes better sense.
- Remember that the object of a preposition is often anarthrous even if the substantive is definite. This is true for the second prepositional phrase, ἐν ὁδῷ δικαιοσύνης, in the excerpt from Matthew 21:32 in sentence 5.
- You may have had trouble sorting out τὰ ἴδια and οἱ ἴδιοι in sentence 6, and you are not alone! The shift from the neuter plural to the masculine plural is a key interpretive issue in this verse from John's Gospel. Some commentators suggest that the neuter refers to the world in general, whereas the masculine refers specifically to the Jewish people. A good commentary will outline the interpretive options and the significance of each option for understanding this verse and the context in which it occurs.

chapter ELEVEN

PASSIVES AND CONDITIONALS

You should complete these assignments after you have studied the material for chapter 11 in the textbook and memorized the required vocabulary, paradigms, and principal parts. Remember that when you encounter a verb form whose lexical form you do not immediately recognize, try to think through the principal parts that you know to see if you can identify the verb. If you still do not recognize the verb, then you may consult the "Principal Parts Chart" (in appendix 14 in the textbook). Once you have completed these assignments to the best of your ability, check your work with the answer key.

For each of the following Greek forms, write out the specified components. Be sure to list all possibilities when applicable. Remember to indicate if a component does not apply for the inflected form by writing any of the following: N/A, n/a, or --.

inflected form	tense	voice	mood	pers	case	num	gender	lexical form	inflected meaning
ἐλογίσθη									
ἐχάρημεν									
ἐθαυμάσθη									
διδάσκῃ									
συνήχθησαν									
εὐηγγελίζοντο									
ἀπελύθησαν									
προσηύχετο									
εὑρίσκομαι									
ἐγενήθη									

TRANSLATION

- For each of the following sentences, double underline each finite verb.
- Above each genitival modifier, write GM and draw an arrow from the genitival modifier to its head noun.
- Put brackets around every [prepositional phrase].
- Single underline each adjective and each pronoun other than a relative pronoun.
- Above each adjective write its function: attributive (ATTR), substantival (SUB), or predicate (PRED).
- Highlight each subordinating conjunction and relative pronoun.
- Put a parenthesis around each (subordinate clause) or (relative clause).
- If applicable, draw an arrow from each relative pronoun to its antecedent.
- Translate the following sentences.

Pop-Up Lexicon

ἀπάγω	I lead away; I am misled (pass)
Φίλιππος, ου, ὁ	Philip

1. ὅτε δὲ ἐπίστευσαν τῷ Φιλίππῳ, . . . ἐβαπτίζοντο.

2. Χριστὸς κηρύσσεται ὅτι ἐκ νεκρῶν ἠγέρθη.

3. καὶ ὡς ἐγένετο ἡμέρα, συνήχθη τὸ πρεσβυτέριον τοῦ λαοῦ, . . . καὶ ἀπήγαγον αὐτὸν εἰς τὸ συνέδριον αὐτῶν.

4. καὶ ἡ γράφη ἠνοίχθη, ἥ ἐστιν τῆς ζωῆς, καὶ ἐκρίθησαν οἱ νεκροὶ κατὰ τὰ ἔργα αὐτῶν.

5. ἐπίστευσεν δὲ Ἀβραὰμ τῷ θεῷ, καὶ ἐλογίσθη αὐτῷ εἰς δικαιοσύνην καὶ φίλος θεοῦ ἐκλήθη.

6. οὐδὲ γὰρ ἐγὼ παρ' ἀνθρώπου παρέλαβον αὐτὸ οὔτε ἐδιδάχθην, ἀλλὰ διὰ τοῦ λογοῦ Ἰησοῦ Χριστοῦ.

7. ὅτε οὖν ἐξῆλθεν, λέγει Ἰησοῦς, νῦν ἐδοξάσθη ὁ υἱὸς τοῦ ἀνθρώπου καὶ ὁ θεὸς ἐδοξάσθη ἐν αὐτῷ.

CORRECTION AND ASSESSMENT

Instructions

Once you have completed the above translation exercises to the best of your ability, you may then look at the answer key. On this page, you will find spaces to assess any mistakes you made and to indicate the course of action you took to address the problem.

inflected form or sentence #	assessment	course of action

ANSWER KEY

Parsing

inflected form	tense	voice	mood	pers	case	num	gender	lexical form	inflected meaning
ἐλογίσθη	aor	pass	ind	3rd	n/a	sg	n/a	λογίζομαι	he/she/it was thought
ἐχάρημεν	aor	pass	ind	1st	n/a	pl	n/a	χαίρω	we rejoiced
ἐθαυμάσθη	aor	pass	ind	3rd	n/a	sg	n/a	θαυμάζω	he/she/it was amazed
διδάσκῃ	pres	mid pass	ind	2nd	n/a	sg	n/a	διδάσκω	you (sg) teach for yourself you (sg) are taught
συνήχθησαν	aor	pass	ind	3rd	n/a	pl	n/a	συνάγω	they were gathered
εὐηγγελίζοντο	impf	mid pass	ind	3rd	n/a	pl	n/a	εὐαγγελίζω	they were preaching the gospel for themselves they were being preached [to]
ἀπελύθησαν	aor	pass	ind	3rd	n/a	pl	n/a	ἀπολύω	they were released
προσηύχετο	impf	mid	ind	3rd	n/a	sg	n/a	προσεύχομαι	he/she/it was praying
εὑρίσκομαι	pres	mid pass	ind	1st	n/a	sg	n/a	εὑρίσκω	I find for myself I am found
ἐγενήθη	aor	pass	ind	3rd	n/a	sg	n/a	γίνομαι	he/she/it was made

Additional Notes:

- The form συνήχθησαν could also be understood to have an active, intransitive meaning; we will discuss this in chapter 14.
- The passive form εὐηγγελίζοντο requires an additional preposition in translation per English syntax.

Translation

1. (ὅτε δὲ ἐπίστευσαν τῷ Φιλίππῳ), . . . ἐβαπτίζοντο (Acts 8:12)

   And when they believed Philip, . . . they were baptized.

2. Χριστὸς κηρύσσεται (ὅτι [ἐκ νεκρῶν] ἠγέρθη) (cf. 1 Cor 15:12)

   SUB

   Christ is preached because he was raised from the dead.

3. καὶ ὡς ἐγένετο ἡμέρα, συνήχθη τὸ πρεσβυτέριον τοῦ λαοῦ . . . καὶ ἀπήγαγον αὐτὸν [εἰς τὸ συνέδριον αὐτῶν]. (Luke 22:66)

   GM GM

   And as the day came, the elders of the people gathered . . . and they took him away to their council.

SUB GM

4. καὶ ἡ γράφη ἠνοίχθη, (ἥ ἐστιν τῆς ζωῆς), καὶ ἐκρίθησαν οἱ νεκροὶ [κατὰ τὰ ἔργα αὐτῶν]. (cf. Rev 20:12)

And the Scripture was opened, which is [the Scripture] of life, and the dead were judged according to their works.

SUB GM

5. ἐπίστευσεν δὲ Ἀβραὰμ τῷ θεῷ, καὶ ἐλογίσθη αὐτῷ [εἰς δικαιοσύνην] καὶ φίλος θεοῦ ἐκλήθη (Jas 2:23)

And Abraham believed God, and it was counted to him as righteousness and he was called a friend of God.

GM

6. οὐδὲ γὰρ ἐγὼ [παρ᾽ ἀνθρώπου] παρέλαβον αὐτὸ οὔτε ἐδιδάχθην ἀλλὰ [διὰ τοῦ λογοῦ Ἰησοῦ Χριστοῦ] (cf. Gal 1:12)

For I myself neither received it from a human nor was I taught [it], but [I received it] through the word of Jesus Christ.

GM

7. (ὅτε οὖν ἐξῆλθεν), λέγει Ἰησοῦς, νῦν ἐδοξάσθη ὁ υἱὸς τοῦ ἀνθρώπου καὶ ὁ θεὸς ἐδοξάσθη [ἐν αὐτῷ] (John 13:31)

Therefore, when he went out, Jesus said, "Now the son of man is glorified, and God is glorified in him."

Additional Notes:

- Notice that the direct object of πιστεύω is in the dative case in sentences 1 and 5. We will discuss this further in chapter 14.
- Sentence 4 contains a good example of ellipsis; ἡ γράφη is assumed (but not repeated) in the relative clause ἥ ἐστιν τῆς ζωῆς. Revelation 20:12 uses βιβλίον here instead of γράφη, but you haven't been assigned this word yet.
- Sentence 6 contains another good example of ellipsis; the verb παρέλαβον is assumed (but not repeated) in the clause beginning with ἀλλά, as indicated with the square brackets. Also, in English the verb "to teach" in this context requires an object, which is indicated in the square brackets.
- In sentence 7, notice how the present tense form λέγει is translated in the narrative context of John 13—the translation "said" reflects the fact that English has a time-based verbal system; "Jesus says" in this context would be awkward in English.
- In sentence 7, notice also the translation of the two aorist passives; a past-tense rendering of these verbs would not accurately reflect the Greek. At this point in the narrative, Judas has just left to betray Jesus. Jesus knows that the events are set in motion that will lead to his crucifixion, which in John's Gospel is associated with glory. It would even be possible to understand these two aorist passives as having a future reference and to translate them as follows: "Now the son of man will be glorified, and God will be glorified in him." This is another example of the need to pay careful attention to the overall context when considering how Greek verbs are functioning and how best to translate them.

chapter **TWELVE**

THIRD DECLENSION PARADIGMS:

The Rest of Nouns and Adjectives; More Pronouns (Interrogative and Indefinite)

You should complete these assignments after you have studied the material for chapter 12 in the textbook and memorized the required vocabulary, paradigms, and principal parts. Remember that when you encounter a verb form whose lexical form you do not immediately recognize, try to think through the principal parts that you know to see if you can identify the verb. If you still do not recognize the verb, then you may consult the "Principal Parts Chart" (in appendix 14 in the textbook). Once you have completed these assignments to the best of your ability, check your work with the answer key.

For each of the following Greek forms, write out the specified components. Be sure to list all possibilities when applicable. Remember to indicate if a component does not apply for the inflected form by writing any of the following: N/A, n/a, or --.

inflected form	tense	voice	mood	pers	case	num	gender	lexical form	inflected meaning
ἔθνει									
ὀνόματα									
χάριν									
πίστει									
ὕδατα									
οὐδέν									
νύκτας									
ὠτός									
σαρξί									
ποδῶν									

TRANSLATION

- For each of the following sentences, double underline each finite verb.
- Above each genitival modifier, write GM and draw an arrow from the genitival modifier to its head noun.
- Put brackets around every [prepositional phrase].
- Single underline each adjective and each pronoun other than a relative pronoun.
- Above each adjective write its function: attributive (ATTR), substantival (SUB), or predicate (PRED).
- Highlight each subordinating conjunction and relative pronoun.
- Put a parenthesis around each (subordinate clause) or (relative clause).
- If applicable, draw an arrow from each relative pronoun to its antecedent.
- Translate the following sentences.

Pop-Up Lexicon

ὀφθαλμός, οῦ, ὁ eye, sight

1. ὑμῶν δὲ μακάριοι οἱ ὀφθαλμοὶ ὅτι βλέπουσιν καὶ τὰ ὦτα ὑμῶν ὅτι ἀκούουσιν.

2. καὶ ὃς . . . δέχεται ἓν παιδίον . . . ἐπὶ τῷ ὀνόματί μου, ἐμὲ δέχεται.

3. καὶ . . . οἱ Φαρισαῖοι ἔλεγον τοῖς μαθηταῖς αὐτοῦ· διὰ τί μετὰ τῶν τελωνῶν καὶ ἁμαρτωλῶν ἐσθίει ὁ διδάσκαλος ὑμῶν;

4. ἐλάμβανον πνεῦμα ἅγιον.

5. τοῦτο τὸ ποτήριον ἡ καινὴ διαθήκη ἐστὶν ἐν τῷ ἐμῷ αἵματι.

6. κύριος κυρίων ἐστὶν καὶ βασιλεὺς βασιλέων.

---

7. τῇ γὰρ ἐλπίδι ἐσώθημεν . . . ὃ γὰρ βλέπει τίς πιστεύει;

---

8. ἤκουσαν δὲ οἱ ἀπόστολοι . . . ὅτι καὶ τὰ ἔθνη ἐδέξαντο τὸν λόγον τοῦ θεοῦ.

CORRECTION AND ASSESSMENT

Instructions

Once you have completed the above translation exercises to the best of your ability, you may then look at the answer key. On this page, you will find spaces to assess any mistakes you made and to indicate the course of action you took to address the problem.

inflected form or sentence #	assessment	course of action

ANSWER KEY

Parsing

inflected form	tense	voice	mood	pers	case	num	gender	lexical form	inflected meaning
ἔθνει	n/a	n/a	n/a	n/a	dat	sg	neut	ἔθνος, -ους, τό	to/by/with/in nation
ὀνόματα	n/a	n/a	n/a	n/a	nom acc	pl	neut	ὄνομα, -ματος, τό	names
χάριν	n/a	n/a	n/a	n/a	acc	sg	fem	χάρις, -ιτος, ἡ	grace
πίστει	n/a	n/a	n/a	n/a	dat	sg	fem	πίστις, -εως, ἡ	to/by/with/in faith
ὕδατα	n/a	n/a	n/a	n/a	nom acc	pl	neut	ὕδωρ, ὕδατος, τό	water(s)
οὐδέν	n/a	n/a	n/a	n/a	nom acc	sg	neut	οὐδείς, οὐδεμία, οὐδέν	nothing
νύκτας	n/a	n/a	n/a	n/a	acc	pl	fem	νύξ, νυκτός, ἡ	nights
ὠτός	n/a	n/a	n/a	n/a	gen	sg	neut	οὖς, ὠτός, τό	of an ear
σαρξί	n/a	n/a	n/a	n/a	dat	pl	fem	σάρξ, σαρκός, ἡ	to/by/with/in bodies
ποδῶν	n/a	n/a	n/a	n/a	gen	pl	masc	πούς, ποδός, ὁ	of feet

Translation

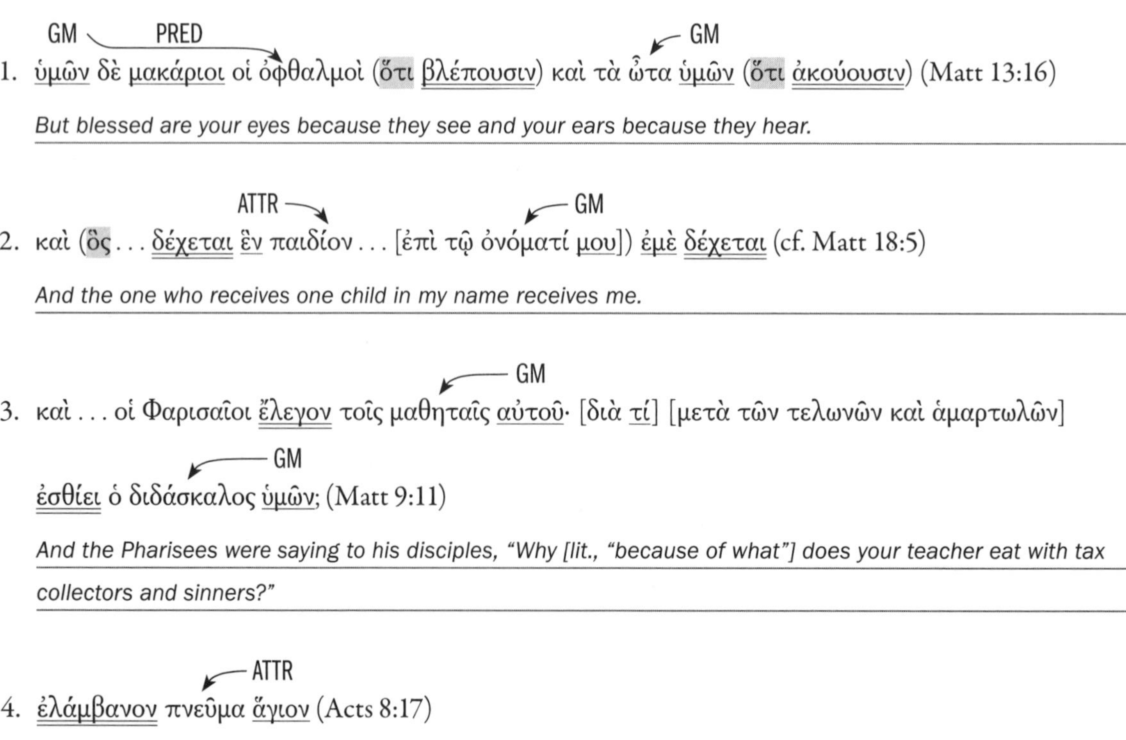

GM PRED GM

1. ὑμῶν δὲ μακάριοι οἱ ὀφθαλμοὶ (ὅτι βλέπουσιν) καὶ τὰ ὦτα ὑμῶν (ὅτι ἀκούουσιν) (Matt 13:16)

   But blessed are your eyes because they see and your ears because they hear.

ATTR GM

2. καὶ (ὃς . . . δέχεται ἓν παιδίον . . . [ἐπὶ τῷ ὀνόματί μου]) ἐμὲ δέχεται (cf. Matt 18:5)

   And the one who receives one child in my name receives me.

GM

3. καὶ . . . οἱ Φαρισαῖοι ἔλεγον τοῖς μαθηταῖς αὐτοῦ· [διὰ τί] [μετὰ τῶν τελωνῶν καὶ ἁμαρτωλῶν]

   GM

   ἐσθίει ὁ διδάσκαλος ὑμῶν; (Matt 9:11)

   And the Pharisees were saying to his disciples, "Why [lit., "because of what"] does your teacher eat with tax collectors and sinners?"

ATTR

4. ἐλάμβανον πνεῦμα ἅγιον (Acts 8:17)

   ~~*I was receiving the Holy Spirit.*~~

   They were receiving the Holy Spirit.

ATTR ATTR ATTR

5. τοῦτο τὸ ποτήριον ἡ καινὴ διαθήκη ἐστὶν [ἐν τῷ ἐμῷ αἵματι] (1 Cor 11:25)

   This cup is the new covenant with my blood.

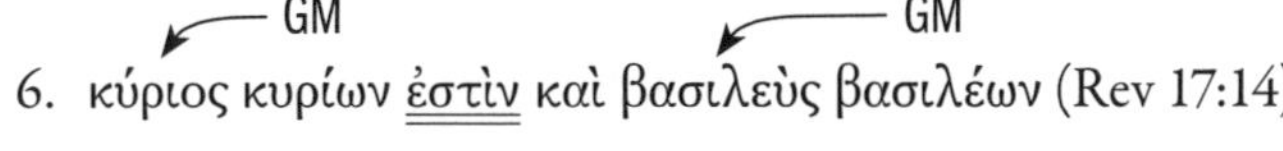

6. κύριος κυρίων ἐστὶν καὶ βασιλεὺς βασιλέων (Rev 17:14)

He is Lord of lords and the king of kings.

7. τῇ γὰρ ἐλπίδι ἐσώθημεν . . . (ὃ γὰρ βλέπει) τίς πιστεύει; (cf. Rom 8:24)

For we were saved in hope . . . for who believes [in] what he sees?

GM

8. ἤκουσαν δὲ οἱ ἀπόστολοι . . . (ὅτι καὶ τὰ ἔθνη ἐδέξαντο τὸν λόγον τοῦ θεοῦ). (Acts 11:1)

And the apostles heard . . . that gentiles also received the word of God.

Additional Notes:

- In sentence 2, notice that the adjective ἕν is functioning almost like the indefinite pronoun τις, τι. This is common in the GNT, although this verse has been modified from the original.
- In sentence 3, the expression διὰ τί is an idiom meaning "why?" You might have figured that out with a literalistic rendering of "because of what?" or "on account of what?"
- In sentence 4, as we have seen before, the context makes clear that a first-person singular is not intended, so it has been crossed out. Instead, a third-person plural is the correct parsing for ἐλάμβανον.
- You may remember from the translations in chapter 5 that in sentence 6 here (Rev 17:14), the subject "he" is understood from the larger context.
- In sentence 7, there is no antecedent for the relative pronoun, which is functioning as the object of the verb βλέπει ("he sees *what*"). If you had trouble with this verse, don't be discouraged—it is deceptively difficult.
- You might have wondered how to translate καί in sentence 8. Remember that when καί appears between two (or more) syntactic units that are not the same (e.g., a conjunction and a noun phrase) then it is best translated as "even" or "also." This is the ascensive function of the conjunction καί.

chapter THIRTEEN

THE PRESENT PARTICIPLE AND PARTICIPLE BASICS

You should complete these assignments after you have studied the material for chapter 13 in the textbook and memorized the required vocabulary, paradigms, and principal parts. Remember that when you encounter a verb form whose lexical form you do not immediately recognize, try to think through the principal parts that you know to see if you can identify the verb. If you still do not recognize the verb, then you may consult the "Principal Parts Chart" (in appendix 14 in the textbook). Once you have completed these assignments to the best of your ability, check your work with the answer key.

For each of the following Greek forms, write out the specified components. Be sure to list all possibilities when applicable. Remember to indicate if a component does not apply for the inflected form by writing any of the following: N/A, n/a, or --.

inflected form	tense	voice	mood	pers	case	num	gender	lexical form	inflected meaning
ἀγοράζοντας									
εὑρίσκοντες									
ἐγγίζουσαν									
πίνων									
πορευόμενον									
φέρον									
πεμπομένοις									
σῳζομένους									
πιστεύουσιν									
δεχόμενος									

TRANSLATION

- For each of the following sentences, double underline each finite verb.
- Put brackets around every [prepositional phrase].
- Single underline each adjective.[1]
- Above each adjective write its function: attributive (ATTR), substantival (SUB), or predicate (PRED).
- Highlight each subordinating conjunction and relative pronoun.
- Put a parenthesis around each (subordinate clause) or (relative clause).
- If applicable, draw an arrow from each relative pronoun to its antecedent.
- Put a square box around every participle.
- Above each participle write its function: adverbial (ADV), attributive (ATTR), or substantival (SUB).
- If applicable, draw an arrow from the participle to the word it modifies.
- Translate the following sentences.

Pop-Up Lexicon

μείζων, -ον	greater, greatest
νόσος, -ου, ἡ	disease, illness
παραλυτικός, -ή, -όν	lame; lame person, paralytic (subst)
περιάγω	I lead around, I take about, I go around
Σαμαρίτης, -ου, ὁ	Samaritan

1. διαμαρτυράμενοι . . . τὸν λόγον τοῦ κυρίου ὑπέστρεφον εἰς Ἱεροσόλυμα, πολλάς τε πόλεις τῶν Σαμαριτῶν εὐηγγελίζοντο.

2. διὰ τοῦτο ἐν παραβολαῖς αὐτοῖς λέγω, ὅτι βλέποντες οὐ βλέπουσιν καὶ ἀκούοντες οὐκ ἀκούουσιν.

3. Ἰησοῦς δὲ ἔκραξεν καὶ εἶπεν, ὁ πιστεύων εἰς ἐμὲ οὐ πιστεύει εἰς ἐμὲ ἀλλ' εἰς τὸν ἀποστέλλοντά με, καὶ ὁ βλέπων ἐμὲ βλέπει τὸν ἀποστέλλοντά με.

1. Notice that from now on, you no longer need to identify genitival modifiers and pronouns other than relative pronouns. At this point, you should be able to identify them easily.

4. καὶ περιῆγεν ἐν ὅλῃ τῇ Γαλιλαίᾳ διδάσκων ἐν ταῖς συναγωγαῖς αὐτῶν καὶ κηρύσσων τὸ εὐαγγέλιον τῆς βασιλείας καὶ θεραπεύων πᾶσαν νόσον . . . ἐν τῷ λαῷ.

5. καὶ ἔρχονται φέροντες πρὸς αὐτὸν παραλυτικὸν αἰρόμενον ὑπὸ τεσσάρων.

6. ἦλθεν γὰρ Ἰωάννης μὴ ἐσθίων μήδε πίνων, καὶ λέγουσιν, δαιμόνιον ἔχει.

7. ὁ μὴ ὢν μετ᾽ ἐμοῦ κατ᾽ ἐμοῦ ἐστιν.

8. καὶ . . . ἐπορεύετο ἐνώπιον ἀναβαίνων εἰς Ἱεροσόλυμα.

9. ἐν ἐκείνῃ τῇ ὥρᾳ προσῆλθον οἱ μαθηταὶ τῷ Ἰησοῦ λέγοντες, τίς ἄρα μείζων ἐστὶν ἐν τῇ βασιλείᾳ τῶν οὐρανῶν;

CORRECTION AND ASSESSMENT

Instructions

Once you have completed the above translation exercises to the best of your ability, you may then look at the answer key. On this page, you will find spaces to assess any mistakes you made and to indicate the course of action you took to address the problem.

inflected form or sentence #	assessment	course of action

ANSWER KEY

Parsing

inflected form	tense	voice	mood	pers	case	num	gender	lexical form	inflected meaning
ἀγοράζοντας	pres	act	ptc	n/a	acc	pl	masc	ἀγοράζω	ones who buy
εὑρίσκοντες	pres	act	ptc	n/a	nom	pl	masc	εὑρίσκω	ones who find
ἐγγίζουσαν	pres	act	ptc	n/a	acc	sg	fem	ἐγγίζω	one who approaches
πίνων	pres	act	ptc	n/a	nom	sg	masc	πίνω	one who drinks
πορευόμενον	pres	mid	ptc	n/a	acc nom acc	sg	masc neut neut	πορεύομαι	one who goes that which goes that which goes
φέρον	pres	act	ptc	n/a	nom acc	sg	neut	φέρω	that which bears
πεμπομένοις	pres	mid pass	ptc	n/a	dat	pl	masc neut masc neut	πέμπω	to/by/with/in them who/which send for themselves to/by/with/in them who/which are sent
σῳζομένους	pres	mid pass	ptc	n/a	acc	pl	masc	σῴζω	ones who save for themselves ones who are saved

inflected form	tense	voice	mood	pers	case	num	gender	lexical form	inflected meaning
πιστεύουσιν	pres	act	ind ptc ptc	3rd n/a n/a	n/a dat dat	pl pl pl	n/a masc neut	πιστεύω	they believe to/by/with/in them who believe to/by/with/in those which believe
δεχόμενος	pres	mid	ptc	n/a	nom	sg	masc	δέχομαι	one who receives

Additional Notes:

- You will notice that all participles have been translated as substantival participles and generally use "one(s)." If these were attributive or adverbial participles, then they could not be translated this way. It should be evident by now, however, that these inflected meanings would likely be changed based on the context in which they occured.

Translation

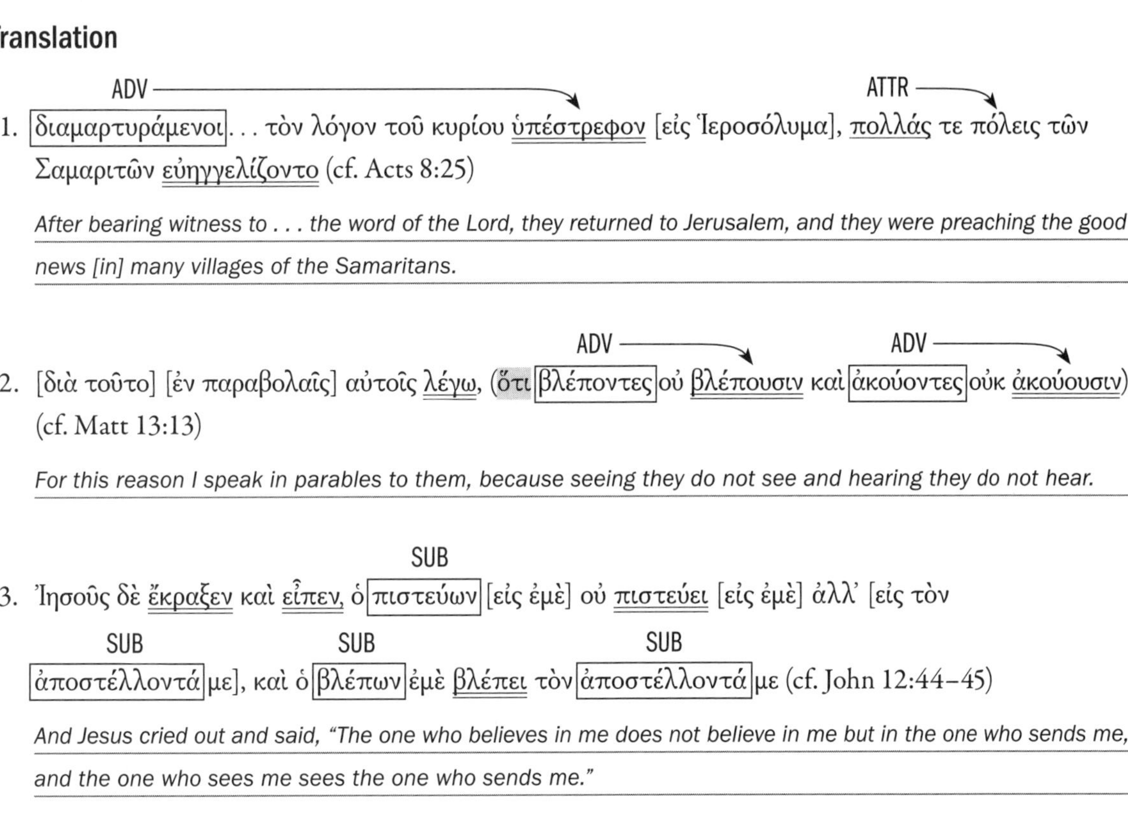

1. διαμαρτυράμενοι . . . τὸν λόγον τοῦ κυρίου ὑπέστρεφον [εἰς Ἱεροσόλυμα], πολλάς τε πόλεις τῶν Σαμαριτῶν εὐηγγελίζοντο (cf. Acts 8:25)

   After bearing witness to . . . the word of the Lord, they returned to Jerusalem, and they were preaching the good news [in] many villages of the Samaritans.

2. [διὰ τοῦτο] [ἐν παραβολαῖς] αὐτοῖς λέγω, (ὅτι βλέποντες οὐ βλέπουσιν καὶ ἀκούοντες οὐκ ἀκούουσιν) (cf. Matt 13:13)

   For this reason I speak in parables to them, because seeing they do not see and hearing they do not hear.

3. Ἰησοῦς δὲ ἔκραξεν καὶ εἶπεν, ὁ πιστεύων [εἰς ἐμὲ] οὐ πιστεύει [εἰς ἐμὲ] ἀλλ' [εἰς τὸν ἀποστέλλοντά με], καὶ ὁ βλέπων ἐμὲ βλέπει τὸν ἀποστέλλοντά με (cf. John 12:44–45)

   And Jesus cried out and said, "The one who believes in me does not believe in me but in the one who sends me, and the one who sees me sees the one who sends me."

4. καὶ περιῆγεν [ἐν ὅλῃ τῇ Γαλιλαίᾳ] διδάσκων [ἐν ταῖς συναγωγαῖς αὐτῶν] καὶ κηρύσσων τὸ εὐαγγέλιον τῆς βασιλείας καὶ θεραπεύων πᾶσαν νόσον . . . [ἐν τῷ λαῷ]. (Matt 4:23)

   And he went around the whole [of] Galilee, teaching in their synagogues and preaching the good news of the kingdom and healing every type [of] disease among the people.

ADV ATTR SUB

5. καὶ ἔρχονται φέροντες [πρὸς αὐτὸν] παραλυτικὸν αἰρόμενον [ὑπὸ τεσσάρων] (Mark 2:3)

And they came bringing to him a paralytic who was carried by four [people].

ADV ADV

6. ἦλθεν γὰρ Ἰωάννης μὴ ἐσθίων μήδε πίνων, καὶ λέγουσιν, δαιμόνιον ἔχει (cf. Matt 11:18)

For John came, neither eating nor drinking, and they said, "He has a demon."

SUB

7. ὁ μὴ ὢν [μετ᾽ ἐμοῦ] [κατ᾽ ἐμοῦ] ἐστιν (Matt 12:30)

The one who is not with me is against me.

ADV

8. καὶ . . . ἐπορεύετο ἐνώπιον ἀναβαίνων [εἰς Ἱεροσόλυμα] (Luke 19:28)

And he was going ahead, ascending to Jerusalem.

ATTR ADV PRED

9. [ἐν ἐκείνῃ τῇ ὥρᾳ] προσῆλθον οἱ μαθηταὶ τῷ Ἰησοῦ λέγοντες, τίς ἄρα μείζων ἐστὶν [ἐν τῇ βασιλείᾳ τῶν οὐρανῶν]; (Matt 18:1)

In that hour the disciples came to Jesus, saying, "Who then is the greatest in the kingdom of heaven?"

Additional Notes:

- In sentence 1, some type of preposition is required after "preaching," such as "in"—this is in square brackets because this concerns English syntax, not Greek.
- The participles in sentence 2 are actually "concessive," which we'll look at in chapter 15. But for now, you may have felt as if you wanted to translate them as follows: "Although seeing, they do not see and although hearing, they do not hear." If you were thinking along these lines, you are doing well!
- In sentence 4, the use of the adjective ὅλη is best translated as "the whole of" per English usage; this is indicated by the addition of [of] to the translation. In sentence 4, the use of πᾶς is a bit idiomatic. When πᾶς is used attributively with a singular noun, it can indicate "every" or "every kind," "every type," etc. In English, the preposition "of" is required in this context, which is indicated by square brackets.
- In sentence 5, people are clearly implied in the use of τεσσάρων, so you could also translate this as "four people."
- In sentence 9, οὐρανῶν is plural (reflecting Hebrew idiom), but it is not usually translated as a plural in English.

chapter **FOURTEEN**

TEXT FOR INTEGRATION

You can make a copy of this text to accompany your work on the integration exercises for chapter 14 in the textbook.

Pop-Up Lexicon

ἀναλαμβάνω	I take up, I carry
ὁράω	I see, I notice, I perceive
πατήρ, πατρός, ὁ	father, ancestor

Pop-Up Principal Parts

ὁράω, ὄψομαι, εἶδον, ἑώρακα, n/a, ὤφθην

1. εἴ τις πιστεύει Ἰησοῦ, ἤρχετο τὴν βασιλείαν τοῦ θεοῦ.

2. πάντες οἱ πιστεύοντες τῷ ὀνόματι τοῦ υἱοῦ τοῦ ἀνθρώπου οὐ πιστεύουσιν εἰς αὐτὸν

3. ἀλλ᾽ εἰς τὸν πατέρα τὸν ἀποστέλλοντα αὐτόν.

4. μακάριοι οἱ πιστεύοντες εἰς χριστόν, ὅτι αὐτοὶ τὸν θεὸν ἐβλέπον.

5. μακάριοι οἱ βαπτιζόμενοι ὑπὸ τῶν μαθητῶν τουτῶν, ὅτι ἐκαθαρίσθησαν τῇ καρδίᾳ αὐτῶν.

6. καὶ ἀληθής ἐστιν ἡ τῶν ἀποστόλων μαρτυρία

7. ὃς ἠγέρθη ἐν σαρκί,

8. διεμαρτυρήθη ἐν πνεύματι,

9. ὤφθη ἀγγέλοις,

10. ἐκηρύχθη ἐν ἔθνεσιν,

11. ἐπιστεύθη ἐν κόσμῳ,

12. ἀνελήμφθη ἐν δόξῃ.

chapter FIFTEEN

THE AORIST PARTICIPLE AND ADDITIONAL PARTICIPLE FUNCTIONS

You should complete these assignments after you have studied the material for chapter 15 of the textbook and memorized the required vocabulary, paradigms, and principal parts. Remember that when you encounter a verb form whose lexical form you do not immediately recognize, try to think through the principal parts that you know to see if you can identify the verb. If you still do not recognize the verb, then you may consult the "Principal Parts Chart" (in appendix 14 in the textbook). Once you have completed these assignments to the best of your ability, check your work with the answer key.

For each of the following Greek forms, write out the specified components. Be sure to list all possibilities when applicable. Remember to indicate if a component does not apply for the inflected form by writing any of the following: N/A, n/a, or --.

inflected form	tense	voice	mood	pers	case	num	gender	lexical form	inflected meaning
καταβάς									
ἐλθόντες									
πιστεύσασιν									
παραλαβόντα									
πορευθέντες									
ὑποστρέψασαι									
ἔχουσα									
εὐαγγελισάμενοι									
καθίσασι									
δεξαμένη									

TRANSLATION

- For each of the following sentences, double underline each finite verb.
- Put brackets around every [prepositional phrase].
- Single underline each adjective.
- Above each adjective write its function: attributive (ATTR), substantival (SUB), or predicate (PRED).
- Highlight each subordinating conjunction and relative pronoun.
- Put a parenthesis around each (subordinate clause) or (relative clause).
- If applicable, draw an arrow from each relative pronoun to its antecedent.
- Put a square box around every participle.
- Above each participle write its function: adverbial (ADV), attributive (ATTR), or substantival (SUB).
- If applicable, draw an arrow from the participle to the word it modifies.
- Translate the following sentences.

Pop-Up Lexicon

λίθος, -ου, ὁ	stone
Μαγδαληνή, -ῆς, ἡ	a female inhabitant of Magdala; Magdalene
παρρησιάζομαι	I speak freely, I have courage
πρωΐ	early, early in the morning

1. τῇ δὲ μιᾷ τῶν σαββάτων Μαρία ἡ Μαγδαληνὴ ἔρχεται πρωῒ . . . εἰς τὸ μνημεῖον καὶ βλέπει τὸν λίθον ἠρμένον ἐκ τοῦ μνημείου.

2. ἐπιστραφεὶς ὁ Πέτρος βλέπει τὸν μαθητὴν ὃν ἤγεν ὁ Ἰησοῦς ἀκολουθοῦντα.

3. ἐλθὼν δὲ εἰς τὴν συναγωγὴν ἐπαρρησιάζετο ἐπὶ ἡμέρας τρεῖς . . . πείθων τὰ περὶ τῆς βασιλείας τοῦ θεοῦ.

4. καὶ ταῦτα εἰπὼν βλεπόντων αὐτῶν ἐπήρθη . . . ἀπὸ τῶν ὀφθαλμῶν αὐτῶν.

____

5. καὶ ἐγένετο μετὰ ἡμέρας τρεῖς εὗρον αὐτὸν ἐν τῷ ἱερῷ καθεζόμενον ἐν μέσῳ τῶν διδασκάλων καὶ ἀκούοντα αὐτῶν.

____

____

6. βλέψας δὲ τοὺς ὄχλους ἀνέβη εἰς τὸ ὄρος, καὶ καθίσαντος αὐτοῦ προσῆλθαν αὐτῷ οἱ μαθηταὶ αὐτοῦ.

____

____

7. καὶ πάλιν ἀπελθὼν προσηύξατο τὸν αὐτὸν λόγον εἰπών.

____

8. βαπτισθεὶς δὲ ὁ Ἰησοῦς εὐθὺς ἀνέβη ἀπὸ τοῦ ὕδατος· καὶ ἰδοὺ ἠνεῴχθησαν αὐτῷ οἱ οὐρανοί.

____

____

9. καὶ ἡμεῖς πιστεύομεν, διὸ καὶ λέγομεν, γινώσκοντες ὅτι ὁ ἐγείρας τὸν κύριον Ἰησοῦν καὶ ἡμᾶς σὺν Ἰησοῦ ἐγερεῖ.

____

____

CORRECTION AND ASSESSMENT

Instructions

Once you have completed the parsing and translation exercises to the best of your ability, you may then look at the answer key. On this page, you will find spaces to assess any mistakes you made and to indicate the course of action you took to address the problem.

inflected form or sentence #	assessment	course of action

ANSWER KEY

Parsing

inflected form	tense	voice	mood	pers	case	num	gender	lexical form	inflected meaning
καταβάς	aor	act	ptc	n/a	nom	sg	masc	καταβαίνω	one who came down after coming down
ἐλθόντες	aor	act	ptc	n/a	nom	pl	masc	ἔρχομαι	ones who came after coming
πιστεύσασιν	aor	act	ptc	n/a	dat	pl	masc neut	πιστεύω	to/by/with/in ones who believed to/by/with/in those which believed
παραλαβόντα	aor	act	ptc	n/a	acc nom acc	sg pl pl	masc neut neut	παραλαμβάνω	one who took those which took those which took

inflected form	tense	voice	mood	pers	case	num	gender	lexical form	inflected meaning
πορευθέντες	aor	pass	ptc	n/a	nom	pl	masc	πορεύομαι	they who came after coming
ὑποστρέψασαι	aor	act	ptc	n/a	nom	pl	fem	ὑποστρέφω	those who returned after returning
ἔχουσα	pres	act	ptc	n/a	nom	sg	fem	ἔχω	she who has while having
εὐαγγελισάμενοι	aor	mid	ptc	n/a	nom	pl	masc	εὐαγγελίζω	ones who preached the gospel after preaching the gospel
καθίσασι	aor	act	ptc	n/a	dat	pl	masc neut	καθίζω	to/by/with/in them who sat to/by/with/in those which sat
δεξαμένη	aor	mid	ptc	n/a	nom	sg	fem	δέχομαι	she who received after receiving

Additional Notes:

- As you can see from the inflected meanings, we have listed possible translations for both substantival and temporal adverbial functions of participles that are in the nominative case, because most adverbial participles are in the nominative case. For the oblique cases, we have only indicated the possible translation for the substantival function of the participle. The actual context will make clear how the participle is functioning.

Translation

1. [ATTR]
τῇ δὲ μιᾷ τῶν σαββάτων Μαρία ἡ Μαγδαληνὴ ἔρχεται πρωῒ . . . [εἰς τὸ μνημεῖον] καὶ βλέπει τὸν

λίθον ἠρμένον [ἐκ τοῦ μνημείου] (John 20:1)

On the first [day] of the week, Mary the Magdalene came early . . . to the tomb, and she saw that the stone had been taken away from the tomb.

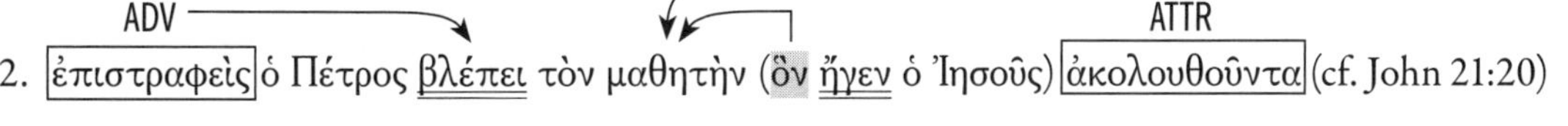

2. ἐπιστραφεὶς ὁ Πέτρος βλέπει τὸν μαθητὴν (ὃν ἤγεν ὁ Ἰησοῦς) ἀκολουθοῦντα (cf. John 21:20)

After Peter turned, he saw the disciple whom Jesus led following.

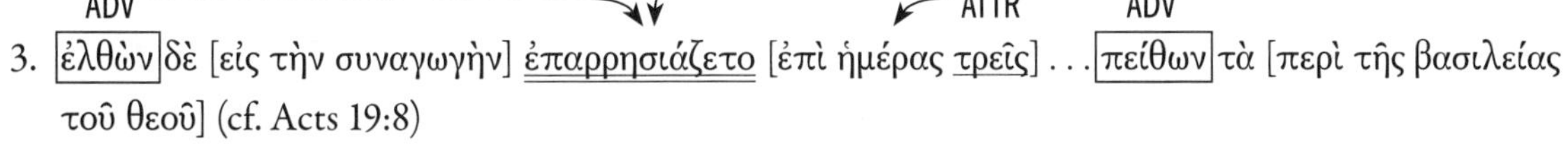

3. ἐλθὼν δὲ [εἰς τὴν συναγωγὴν] ἐπαρρησιάζετο [ἐπὶ ἡμέρας τρεῖς] . . . πείθων τὰ [περὶ τῆς βασιλείας τοῦ θεοῦ] (cf. Acts 19:8)

And after he went into the synagogue, he spoke freely for three days, . . . by persuading [them] of things about the kingdom of God.

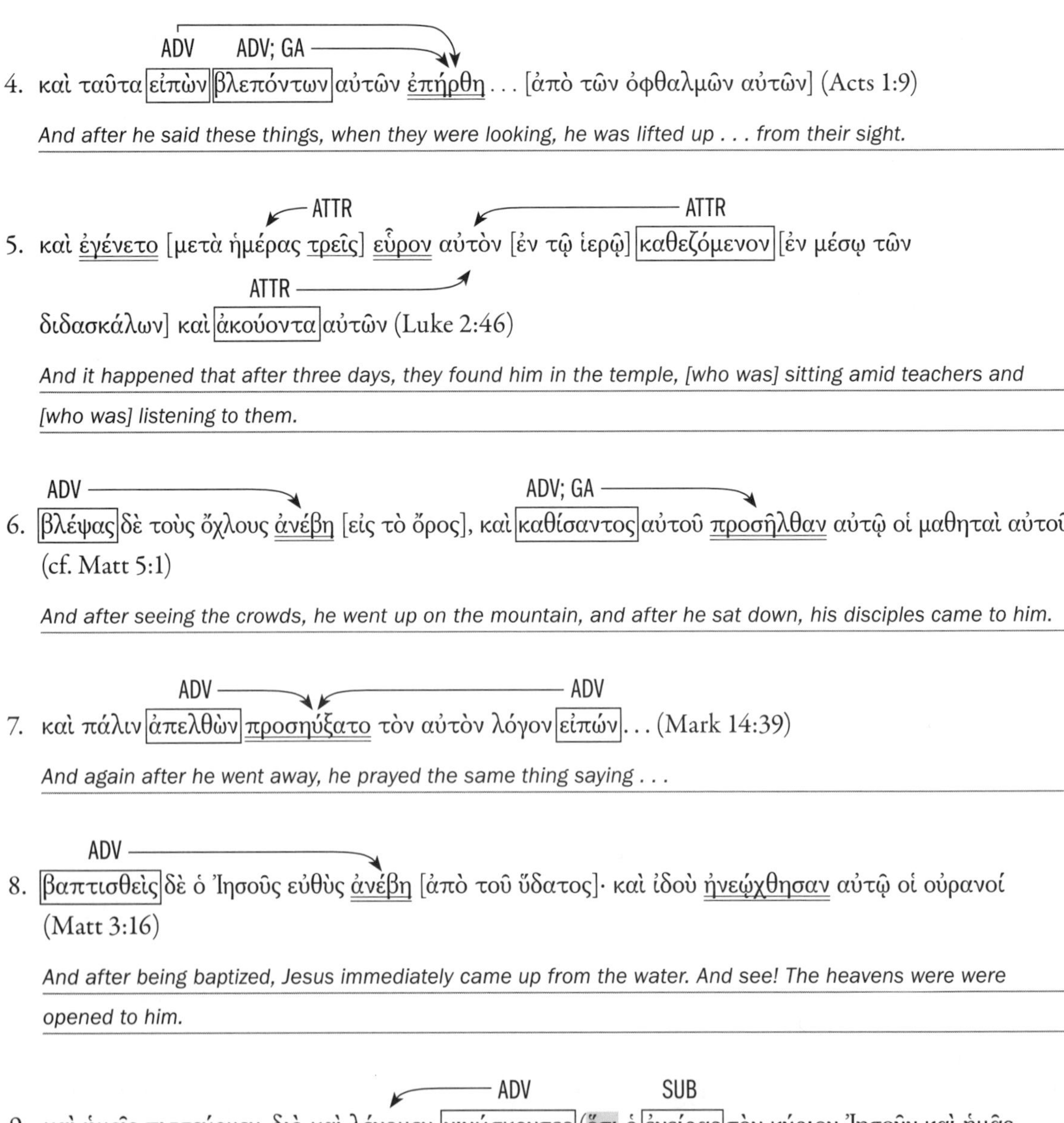

ADV
ADV; GA
4. καὶ ταῦτα εἰπὼν βλεπόντων αὐτῶν ἐπήρθη . . . [ἀπὸ τῶν ὀφθαλμῶν αὐτῶν] (Acts 1:9)
And after he said these things, when they were looking, he was lifted up . . . from their sight.
ATTR
ATTR
5. καὶ ἐγένετο [μετὰ ἡμέρας τρεῖς] εὗρον αὐτὸν [ἐν τῷ ἱερῷ] καθεζόμενον [ἐν μέσῳ τῶν
ATTR
διδασκάλων] καὶ ἀκούοντα αὐτῶν (Luke 2:46)
And it happened that after three days, they found him in the temple, [who was] sitting amid teachers and
[who was] listening to them.
ADV
ADV; GA
6. βλέψας δὲ τοὺς ὄχλους ἀνέβη [εἰς τὸ ὄρος], καὶ καθίσαντος αὐτοῦ προσῆλθαν αὐτῷ οἱ μαθηταὶ αὐτοῦ
(cf. Matt 5:1)
And after seeing the crowds, he went up on the mountain, and after he sat down, his disciples came to him.
ADV
ADV
7. καὶ πάλιν ἀπελθὼν προσηύξατο τὸν αὐτὸν λόγον εἰπών . . . (Mark 14:39)
And again after he went away, he prayed the same thing saying . . .
ADV
8. βαπτισθεὶς δὲ ὁ Ἰησοῦς εὐθὺς ἀνέβη [ἀπὸ τοῦ ὕδατος]· καὶ ἰδοὺ ἠνεῴχθησαν αὐτῷ οἱ οὐρανοί
(Matt 3:16)
And after being baptized, Jesus immediately came up from the water. And see! The heavens were were
opened to him.
ADV
SUB
9. καὶ ἡμεῖς πιστεύομεν, διὸ καὶ λέγομεν, γινώσκοντες (ὅτι ὁ ἐγείρας τὸν κύριον Ἰησοῦν καὶ ἡμᾶς
[σὺν Ἰησοῦ] ἐγερεῖ) (cf. 2 Cor 4:13–14)
And we ourselves believe, therefore we also speak, knowing that the one who raised the Lord Jesus also
raises us with Jesus.

Additional Notes:

- Sentence 1 is a good illustration of the so-called historical present; notice that both present indicatives that occur in this narrative context record events that took place in the past. These verbs are most naturally rendered by simple English past-tense verbs. The adjective μιᾷ is a cardinal, meaning that it indicates how many. Here, however, it is functioning as an ordinal, indicating the first in a series. This is common in the GNT. The noun ἡμέρα is assumed, which is indicated by the square brackets in the English translation and the reason why there are square brackets around ATTR. Also notice that σαββάτων is plural and must be translated according to the overall context. Here it is indicating a week.

- In sentence 1, the participle ἡρμένον is functioning attributively, giving more information about the stone. Hence it parallels the function of a relative clause. In English, this is often rendered by a relative clause that contains a finite verb.
- Sentence 2 also contains another example of a historical present. Notice also that Peter is the subject of the finite verb and thus the logical subject of the participle ἐπιστραφείς, which is reflected in the translation. This participle is a bit unusual in that it is intransitive as an aorist passive, which is also reflected in the translation. In English the placement of participles is important because word order often indicates which word a participle is modifying. In Greek, however, an attributive participle agrees with the substantive that it modifies in case, number, and gender, so ἀκολουθοῦντα could only be modifying τὸν μαθητήν.
- In sentence 2, if you were expecting to read "the disciple whom Jesus loved," you would be right. But you haven't been introduced yet to the Greek verb meaning "to love," so another verb that you should already know has been substituted instead.
- The participle ἐλθών in sentence 3 is a good example of a temporal adverbial participle. As an aorist participle, it indicates an action that took place prior to the action of the main verb. The participle πείθων is also adverbial, but it is functioning as an instrumental participle, indicating *how* the action of the main verb took place. The article τά is functioning substantivally, which is indicated by the translation "things," and is the direct object of the participle πείθων. The prepositional phrase further specifies what those things are. The addition of "them" in square brackets is required by English usage.
- Hopefully you had some fun with sentence 4. The first participle, εἰπών, is nominative singular masculine and is functioning as a temporal adverbial participle indicating an action that took place prior to the main verb. The next participle, βλεπόντων, however, is genitive plural masculine and is part of the genitive absolute construction, βλεπόντων αὐτῶν.
- In sentence 5, both attributive participles are functioning parallel to relative clauses. Translating these participles as such is not really necessary, but we've added that in square brackets so that you can see the Greek syntax reflected a bit more clearly in the English translation.
- In sentence 6, the preposition εἰς can be translated "on," although this less common meaning was not listed when the word was assigned as a vocabulary word.
- Sentence 6 offers another good example of a genitive absolute adverbial participle. Notice that the participle καθίσαντος is genitive singular masculine, so it could not be modifying the main verb προσῆλθαν syntactically. Instead it is providing additional, in this case temporal, information about the main verb προσῆλθαν, namely, Jesus's disciples came to him after he had sat down.
- The use of λόγος in sentence 7 shows the wide semantic range for λόγος; it could be translated "word," but it is really indicating here the content of what Jesus prayed, hence the translation "thing."

chapter SIXTEEN

THE PERFECT AND PLUPERFECT INDICATIVE

You should complete these assignments after you have studied the material for chapter 16 in the textbook and memorized the required vocabulary, paradigms, and principal parts. Once you have completed these assignments to the best of your ability, check your work with the answer key.

For each of the following Greek forms, write out the specified components. Be sure to list all possibilities when applicable. Remember to indicate if a component does not apply for the inflected form by writing any of the following: N/A, n/a, or --.

inflected form	tense	voice	mood	pers	case	num	gender	lexical form	inflected meaning
κεκάθικεν									
δεδόξασμαι									
ἐλήλυθεν									
πέπωκαν									
ἤγγικεν									
δέδεκται									
εἴληφας									
κέκληται									
ἡμαρτήκαμεν									
πεπίστευμαι									

TRANSLATION

- For each of the following sentences, double underline each finite verb.
- Put brackets around every [prepositional phrase].
- Single underline each adjective.
- Above each adjective write its function: attributive (ATTR), substantival (SUB), or predicate (PRED).
- Highlight each subordinating conjunction and relative pronoun.
- Put a parenthesis around each (subordinate clause) or (relative clause).
- If applicable, draw an arrow from each relative pronoun to its antecedent.
- Put a square box around every participle.
- Above each participle write its function: adverbial (ADV), attributive (ATTR), or substantival (SUB).
- If applicable, draw an arrow from the participle to the word it modifies.
- Translate the following sentences.

Pop-Up Lexicon

ἀληθῶς	truly
λαλιά, -ᾶς, ἡ	utterance, speaking
Μεσσίας, -ας, ὁ	Messiah
μονογενής, -ές	unique, only

1. εὑρίσκει οὗτος πρῶτον τὸν ἀδελφὸν τὸν ἴδιον Σίμωνα καὶ λέγει αὐτῷ, εὑρήκαμεν τὸν Μεσσίαν.

2. οὗτός ἐστιν περὶ οὗ γέγραπται ἰδοὺ ἐγὼ ἀποστέλλω τὸν ἄγγελόν μου πρὸ προσώπου σου, ὃς κατασκευάζει τὴν ὁδόν σου ἔμπροσθέν σου.

3. αὕτη δέ ἐστιν ἡ ἀλήθεια ὅτι τὸ φῶς ἐλήλυθεν εἰς τὸν κόσμον.

4. καὶ ὁ πέμψας με πατὴρ ἐκεῖνος εἴρηκεν περὶ ἐμοῦ.

5. τῇ τε γυναικὶ ἔλεγον ὅτι οὐκ διὰ τὴν σὴν λαλιὰν πιστεύομεν, αὐτοὶ γὰρ ἀκηκόαμεν καὶ οἴδαμεν ὅτι οὗτός ἐστιν ἀληθῶς ὁ σωτὴρ τοῦ κόσμου.

6. ὁ λαβὼν αὐτοῦ τὴν μαρτυρίαν ἐσφράγισεν ὅτι ὁ θεὸς ἀληθής ἐστιν.

7. καὶ φωνὴ ἐγένετο ἐκ τῆς νεφέλης λέγουσα, οὗτός ἐστιν ὁ υἱός μου ὁ ἐκλελεγμένος.

8. εἶπεν δὲ πρὸς τὴν γυναῖκα, ἡ πίστις σου σέσωκέν σε.

9. ὁ πιστεύων εἰς αὐτὸν οὐ κρίνεται· ὁ δὲ μὴ πιστεύων ἤδη κέκριται, ὅτι μὴ πεπίστευκεν εἰς τὸ ὄνομα τοῦ μονογενοῦς υἱοῦ τοῦ θεοῦ.

10. καὶ τὰ ἐμὰ πάντα σά ἐστιν καὶ τὰ σὰ ἐμά, καὶ δεδόξασμαι ἐν αὐτοῖς.

CORRECTION AND ASSESSMENT

Instructions

Once you have completed the parsing and translation exercises to the best of your ability, you may then look at the answer key. On this page, you will find spaces to assess any mistakes you made and to indicate the course of action you took to address the problem.

inflected form or sentence #	assessment	course of action

ANSWER KEY

Parsing

inflected form	tense	voice	mood	pers	case	num	gender	lexical form	inflected meaning
κεκάθικεν	pf	act	ind	3rd	n/a	sg	n/a	καθίζω	he/she/it has sat
δεδόξασμαι	pf	mid pass	ind	1st	n/a	sg	n/a	δοξάζω	you (sg) have glorified for yourself you (sg) have been glorifed
ἐλήλυθεν	pf	act	ind	3rd	n/a	sg	n/a	ἔρχομαι	he/she/it has come
πέπωκαν	pf	act	ind	3rd	n/a	pl	n/a	πίνω	they have drunk
ἤγγικεν	pf	act	ind	3rd	n/a	sg	n/a	ἐγγίζω	he/she/it has drawn near

inflected form	tense	voice	mood	pers	case	num	gender	lexical form	inflected meaning
δέδεκται	pf	mid pass	ind	3rd	n/a	sg	n/a	δέχομαι	he/she/it has received for him-/her-/itself he/she/it has been received
εἴληφας	pf	act	ind	2nd	n/a	sg	n/a	λαμβάνω	you (sg) have received
κέκληται	pf	mid pass	ind	3rd	n/a	sg	n/a	καλέω	he/she/it has called for him-/her-/itself he/she/it has been called
ἡμαρτήκαμεν	pf	act	ind	1st	n/a	pl	n/a	ἁμαρτάνω	we have sinned
πεπίστευμαι	pf	mid pass	ind	1st	n/a	sg	n/a	πιστεύω	I have believed for myself I have been believed

Translation

ATTR

1. εὑρίσκει οὗτος πρῶτον τὸν ἀδελφὸν τὸν ἴδιον Σίμωνα καὶ λέγει αὐτῷ, εὑρήκαμεν τὸν Μεσσίαν (John 1:41)

   He [the one] first found his own brother Simon, and he said to him, "We have found the Messiah."

2. οὗτός ἐστιν ([περὶ οὗ] γέγραπται), ἰδοὺ ἐγὼ ἀποστέλλω τὸν ἄγγελόν μου [πρὸ προσώπου σου], (ὃς κατασκευάζει τὴν ὁδόν σου [ἔμπροσθέν σου]) (cf. Matt 11:10)

   This one is [the one] concerning whom it has been written, "See, I myself send my messenger before your face, who prepares your way before you."

3. αὕτη δέ ἐστιν ἡ ἀλήθεια (ὅτι τὸ φῶς ἐλήλυθεν [εἰς τὸν κόσμον]) (cf. John 3:19)

   And this is the truth that the light has come into the world.

ATTR

4. καὶ ὁ πέμψας με πατὴρ ἐκεῖνος εἴρηκεν [περὶ ἐμοῦ] (cf. John 5:37)

   And the Father who sent me, he himself has spoken concerning me.

5. τῇ τε γυναικὶ ἔλεγον (ὅτι οὐκ [διὰ τὴν σὴν λαλιὰν] πιστεύομεν), αὐτοὶ γὰρ ἀκηκόαμεν καὶ οἴδαμεν (ὅτι οὗτός ἐστιν ἀληθῶς ὁ σωτὴρ τοῦ κόσμου) (cf. John 4:42)

   And they were saying to the woman, "We do not believe because of your words, because we ourselves have heard and we know that this is truly the savior of the world."

SUB

6. ὁ λαβὼν αὐτοῦ τὴν μαρτυρίαν ἐσφράγισεν (ὅτι ὁ θεὸς ἀληθής ἐστιν) (John 3:33)

   The one who receives his witness certifies that God is true.

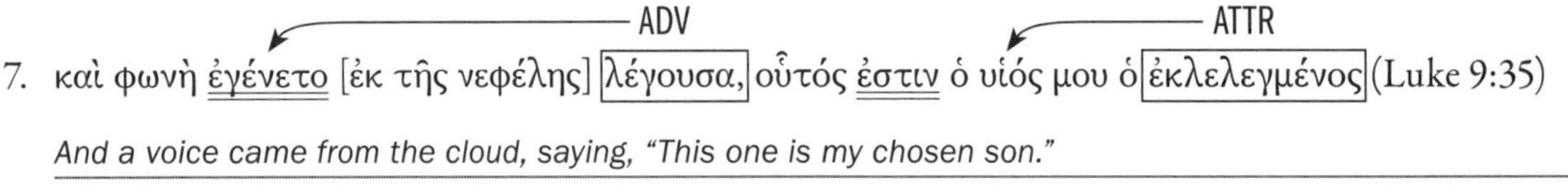

7. καὶ φωνὴ ἐγένετο [ἐκ τῆς νεφέλης] λέγουσα, οὗτός ἐστιν ὁ υἱός μου ὁ ἐκλελεγμένος (Luke 9:35)

And a voice came from the cloud, saying, "This one is my chosen son."

8. εἶπεν δὲ [πρὸς τὴν γυναῖκα], ἡ πίστις σου σέσωκέν σε (Luke 7:50)

And he said to the woman, "Your faith has saved you."

SUB SUB

9. ὁ πιστεύων [εἰς αὐτὸν] οὐ κρίνεται· ὁ δὲ μὴ πιστεύων ἤδη κέκριται, (ὅτι μὴ πεπίστευκεν [εἰς τὸ

ATTR

ὄνομα τοῦ μονογενοῦς υἱοῦ τοῦ θεοῦ]) (John 3:18)

The one who believes in him is not judged; but the one who does not believe has already been judged, because he has not believed in the name of the unique Son of God.

SUB ATTR PRED SUB PRED

10. καὶ τὰ ἐμὰ πάντα σά ἐστιν καὶ τὰ σὰ ἐμά, καὶ δεδόξασμαι [ἐν αὐτοῖς] (John 17:10)

And all things that are mine are yours, and [all things that are] yours [are] mine, and I have been glorified in them.

Additional Notes:

- In John's Gospel, οὗτος frequently functions in a similar way to the third-person personal pronoun, which is reflected in the translation for John 1:41 in sentence 1. This verse also contains two examples of historical presents in a narrative context.
- In sentence 3, ὅτι is functioning to explicate or describe what the truth is (in the original, the word used here pertains to judgment instead of truth; but that word has not yet been assigned); this function of ὅτι is called an "epexegetical" use, and this term can refer to a syntactic unit, such as a ὅτι clause or a participial clause that functions to further explain something.
- In sentence 4, the demonstrative is functioning to add emphasis, which is reflected in the translation. If you translated this as "that one has borne witness . . . ," this is not wrong, but the translation above is more natural English.
- In sentence 5, notice that the first ὅτι is functioning to introduce a quotation, so it is not translated with "that"; instead, quotation marks are used. The second ὅτι is functioning to indicate the content of the verb οἴδαμεν.
- In sentence 7, notice that the participle λέγουσα is feminine because it agrees with the subject φωνή. Also notice that ὁ υἱός μου ὁ ἐκλελεγμένος is a second attributive position construction, which is reflected in the translation.
- In sentence 9, the use of μονογενοῦς in John 3:18 is noteworthy. Many (older) translations have "only begotten," which would suggest that this adjective is from a compounded cognate involving the verb γεννάω, which you will learn later. This verb could be translated, "I beget." But notice that μονογενοῦς has only one nu, indicating that it is not derived from γεννάω. Instead, the adjective μονογενής, -ές is best understood as "unique" or "only."

- The first part of sentence 10 is extremely difficult! The phrase τὰ ἐμὰ πάντα involves the substantival use of the possessive adjective ἐμά; notice that πάντα is in the predicate position functioning to modify ἐμά. The possessive adjective σά is functioning as the predicate adjective of the subject phrase τὰ ἐμὰ πάντα. Then to keep things from getting boring, τὰ σὰ ἐμά is a good example of ellipsis, where the following items in square brackets are assumed but not repeated: τὰ σὰ [πάντα] ἐμά [ἐστιν]. We've added these elliptical items in square brackets for clarity in the English translation. If you figured this one out on your own, be encouraged—you're doing great!

chapter SEVENTEEN

THE PERFECT PARTICIPLE AND MORE PARTICIPLE FUNCTIONS

You should complete these assignments after you have studied the material for chapter 17 in the textbook and memorized the required vocabulary, paradigms, and principal parts. Once you have completed these assignments to the best of your ability, check your work with the answer key.

For each of the following Greek forms, write out the specified components. Be sure to list all possibilities when applicable. Remember to indicate if a component does not apply for the inflected form by writing any of the following: N/A, n/a, or --.

inflected form	tense	voice	mood	pers	case	num	gender	lexical form	inflected meaning
εὐηγγελισμένοι									
εἰδώς									
κρίματος									
γεγονός									
εἰσεληλυθυῖαν									
εἴρηται									
εἰπόντος									
κεκήρυγσθε									
πεπιστευκόσιν									
τεθεραπευμέναι									

TRANSLATION

- For each of the following sentences, double underline each finite verb.
- Put brackets around every [prepositional phrase].
- Single underline each adjective.
- Above each adjective write its function: attributive (ATTR), substantival (SUB), or predicate (PRED).
- Highlight each subordinating conjunction and relative pronoun.
- Put a parenthesis around each (subordinate clause) or (relative clause).
- If applicable, draw an arrow from each relative pronoun to its antecedent.
- Put a square box around every participle.
- Above each participle write its function: adverbial (ADV), attributive (ATTR), or substantival (SUB).
- If applicable, draw an arrow from the participle to the word it modifies.
- Translate the following sentences.

Pop-Up Lexicon

θύρα, -ας, ἡ	door, gate, entrance
Σαμάρεια, -ας, ἡ	Samaria

Pop-Up Principal Parts

μιμνῄσκομαι, -, -, -, μέμνημαι, ἐμνήσθην

γράφω, γράψω, ἔγραψα, γέγραφα, γέγραμμαι, ἐγράφην

1. ταῦτα οὐκ ἔγνωσαν αὐτοῦ οἱ μαθηταὶ τὸ πρῶτον, ἀλλ᾽ ὅτε ἐδοξάσθη Ἰησοῦς τότε ἐμνήσθησαν ὅτι ταῦτα ἦν ἐπ᾽ αὐτῷ γεγραμμένα.

2. ἀκούσαντες δὲ οἱ ἐν Ἱεροσολύμοις ἀπόστολοι ὅτι δέδεκται ἡ Σαμάρεια τὸν λόγον τοῦ θεοῦ, ἀπέστειλαν πρὸς αὐτοὺς Πέτρον καὶ Ἰωάννην.

3. μακάριοι οἱ δεδιωγμένοι ἕνεκεν δικαιοσύνης, ὅτι αὐτῶν ἐστιν ἡ βασιλεία τῶν οὐρανῶν.

4. οὗ γάρ εἰσιν δύο ἢ τρεῖς συνηγμένοι εἰς τὸ ἐμὸν ὄνομα, ἐκεῖ εἰμι ἐν μέσῳ αὐτῶν.

5. εἰδὼς ὁ Ἰησοῦς . . . ὅτι ἀπὸ θεοῦ ἐξῆλθεν καὶ πρὸς τὸν θεὸν ὑπάγει, ἐγείρεται ἐκ τοῦ δείπνου.

6. τῇ γὰρ χάριτί ἐστε σεσῳσμένοι διὰ πίστεως· καὶ τοῦτο οὐκ ἐξ ὑμῶν, θεοῦ τὸ δῶρον· οὐκ ἐξ ἔργων.

7. μετὰ ταῦτα ἔβλεψα, καὶ ἰδοὺ θύρα ἠνεῳγμένη ἐν τῷ οὐρανῷ.

8. καὶ ἦν ἐν τῇ ἐρήμῳ τεσσεράκοντα ἡμέρας πειραζόμενος ὑπὸ τοῦ σατανᾶ, καὶ ἦν μετὰ τῶν θηρίων.

CORRECTION AND ASSESSMENT

Instructions

Once you have completed the parsing and translation to the best of your ability, you may then look at the answer key. On this page, you will find spaces to assess any mistakes you made and to indicate the course of action you took to address the problem.

inflected form or sentence #	assessment	course of action

ANSWER KEY

Parsing

inflected form	tense	voice	mood	pers	case	num	gender	lexical form	inflected meaning
εὐηγγελισμένοι	pf	mid pass	ptc	n/a	nom	pl	masc	εὐαγγελίζω	they who have preached good news for themselves those who have been preached (to)
εἰδώς	pf	act	ptc	n/a	nom	sg	masc	οἶδα	one who has known
κρίματος	n/a	n/a	n/a	n/a	gen	sg	neut	κρίμα, -ατος, τό	of judgment
γεγονός	pf	act	ptc	n/a	nom acc	sg	neut	γίνομαι	that which has become
εἰσεληλυθυῖαν	pf	act	ptc	n/a	acc	sg	fem	ἐξέρχομαι	one (fem) who has entered
εἴρηται	pf	mid pass	ind	3rd	n/a	sg	n/a	λέγω	he/she/it has spoken for himself/herself/itself he/she/it has been spoken (to)
εἰπόντος	aor	act	ptc	n/a	gen	sg	masc	λέγω	of him who spoke

inflected form	tense	voice	mood	pers	case	num	gender	lexical form	inflected meaning
κεκήρυγσθε	pf	mid pass	ind	2nd	n/a	pl	n/a	κηρύσσω	you (pl) have preached for yourselves you (pl) have been preached (to)
πεπιστευκόσιν	pf	act	ptc	n/a	dat	pl	masc neut	πιστεύω	to/by/with/in ones who have believed to/by/with/in those that have believed
τεθεραπευμέναι	pf	mid pass	ptc	n/a	nom	pl	fem	θεραπεύω	they who have healed for themselves they who have been healed

Translation

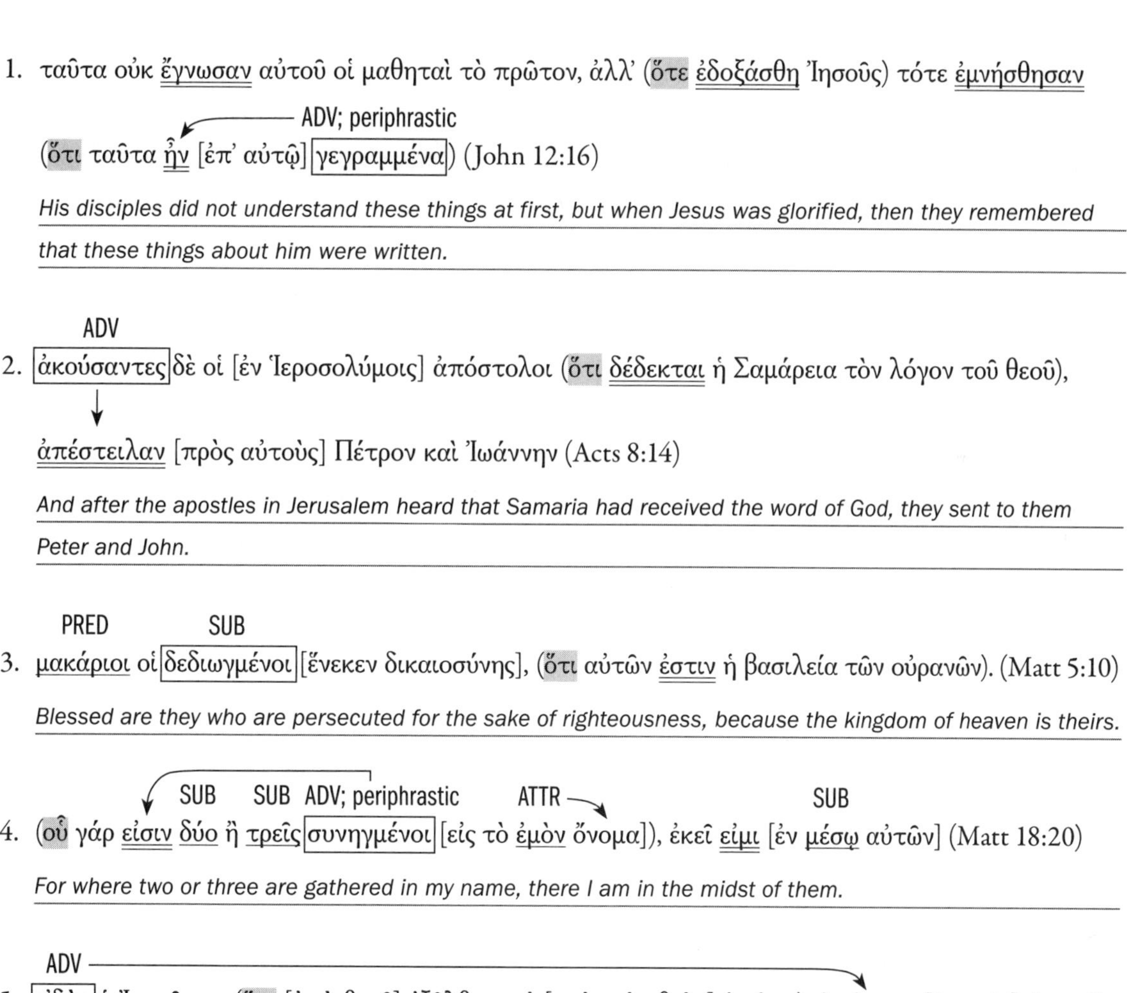

1. ταῦτα οὐκ ἔγνωσαν αὐτοῦ οἱ μαθηταὶ τὸ πρῶτον, ἀλλ' (ὅτε ἐδοξάσθη Ἰησοῦς) τότε ἐμνήσθησαν (ὅτι ταῦτα ἦν [ἐπ' αὐτῷ] γεγραμμένα) (John 12:16)

   ADV; periphrastic

   His disciples did not understand these things at first, but when Jesus was glorified, then they remembered that these things about him were written.

2. ἀκούσαντες δὲ οἱ [ἐν Ἱεροσολύμοις] ἀπόστολοι (ὅτι δέδεκται ἡ Σαμάρεια τὸν λόγον τοῦ θεοῦ), ἀπέστειλαν [πρὸς αὐτοὺς] Πέτρον καὶ Ἰωάννην (Acts 8:14)

   ADV

   And after the apostles in Jerusalem heard that Samaria had received the word of God, they sent to them Peter and John.

3. μακάριοι οἱ δεδιωγμένοι [ἕνεκεν δικαιοσύνης], (ὅτι αὐτῶν ἐστιν ἡ βασιλεία τῶν οὐρανῶν). (Matt 5:10)

   PRED SUB

   Blessed are they who are persecuted for the sake of righteousness, because the kingdom of heaven is theirs.

4. (οὗ γάρ εἰσιν δύο ἢ τρεῖς συνηγμένοι [εἰς τὸ ἐμὸν ὄνομα]), ἐκεῖ εἰμι [ἐν μέσῳ αὐτῶν] (Matt 18:20)

   SUB SUB ADV; periphrastic ATTR SUB

   For where two or three are gathered in my name, there I am in the midst of them.

5. εἰδὼς ὁ Ἰησοῦς . . . (ὅτι [ἀπὸ θεοῦ] ἐξῆλθεν καὶ [πρὸς τὸν θεὸν] ὑπάγει), ἐγείρεται [ἐκ τοῦ δείπνου] (John 13:1, 3–4)

   ADV

   Jesus, knowing . . . that he came from God and he was going to God, rose from the meal.

ADV; periphrastic

6. τῇ γὰρ χάριτί ἐστε σεσῳσμένοι [διὰ πίστεως]· καὶ τοῦτο οὐκ [ἐξ ὑμῶν], θεοῦ τὸ δῶρον· οὐκ [ἐξ ἔργων] (Eph 2:8–9)

For by grace you are saved through faith; and this [is] not from you, [but it is] the gift of God, [and it is] not from works.

ATTR

7. [μετὰ ταῦτα] ἔβλεψα, καὶ ἰδοὺ θύρα ἠνεῳγμένη [ἐν τῷ οὐρανῷ] . . . (cf. Rev 4:1)

After these things I looked, and behold, a door that had been opened in heaven . . .

ATTR ADV; periphrastic

8. καὶ ἦν [ἐν τῇ ἐρήμῳ] τεσσεράκοντα ἡμέρας πειραζόμενος [ὑπὸ τοῦ σατανᾶ], καὶ ἦν [μετὰ τῶν θηρίων] (Mark 1:13)

And in the wilderness for forty days, he was being tempted by Satan, and he was with the wild beasts.

Additional Notes:

- Τὸ πρῶτον in sentence 1 is a good example of an idiomatic use of the adverb πρῶτον. A literal translation, "the first," does not make sense. The fact that this does not make sense should be a good prompt to look this expression up in a lexicon, where you will find glosses such as "at first," "earlier," or even "the first time."
- Ὅτε ἐδοξάσθη Ἰησοῦς in sentence 1 is a good example of a dependent temporal clause.
- Also in sentence 1, the ὅτι clause indicates the content of the verb ἐμνήσθησαν.
- The periphrastic construction ἦν . . . γεγραμμένα corresponds to a pluperfect indicative, which is reflected in the translation "were . . . written." Note also the embedding of the prepositional phrase within the periphrastic construction in sentence 1, which is fairly common.
- In sentence 2, the adverbial participle ἀκούσαντες could be understood as either temporal ("after hearing," "when they heard") or causal ("because they heard"), as there is much overlap between the function of an aorist temporal participle and an aorist causal participle. Notice that Greek participles are often best rendered in English as finite verbs in subordinate clauses.
- In sentence 2, the ὅτι clause indicates the content of the participle ἀκούσαντες.
- In sentence 3, there is no proximate substantive that agrees with the participle δεδιωγμένοι in case, number, and gender, so the participle must be functioning substantivally. Technically, it is also functioning as the subject of the verbless clause in which μακάριοι functions as the predicate adjective, which is reflected in the addition of "are" to the translation.
- The adverb οὗ in sentence 4 should not be confused with the relative pronoun οὗ, which has the same form; the overall context indicates that the adverb is intended.
- In sentence 4, notice that the subject δύο ἢ τρεῖς is embedded in the periphrastic construction εἰσιν . . . συνηγμένοι; this is not unusual.
- In sentence 5, the subject of the main clause, and hence of the main verb, is ὁ Ἰησοῦς, which is indicated in the translation. Notice that the ὅτι clause indicates the content of the participle εἰδώς. Also notice

the use of the historical present, ἐγείρεται, which is best rendered as an English simple past in this narrative context.

- The periphrastic construction ἐστε σεσῳσμένοι in sentence 6 could also be rendered "you have been saved" in English.
- The antecedent of the demonstrative pronoun τοῦτο in sentence 6 is not explicitly stated, but refers more generally to the overall discussion of salvation. This is sometimes referred to as a "neuter of general reference."
- Notice the multiple occurrences of ellipsis in sentence 6, where a form of εἰμί is understood, which is indicated by square brackets in the translation.
- In sentence 7, the attributive participle ἠνεῳγμένη is modifying the substantive θύρα. Notice the subtlety of this attributive participle. If this construction is rendered "an open door," that has a different connotation than "a door that had been opened." In apocalyptic literature, the image of a door to heaven being opened is fairly common. The implication here is that God is supernaturally revealing something to the seer, in this case John, that could not be perceived by human observation. Many English translations (e.g., ESV, NIV, NKJV, NASB) try to capture this nuance with "a door standing open."
- There is no rule as to how many additional words or syntactic units can be embedded in a periphrastic construction. In the example from sentence 8 (Mark 1:13), the periphrastic construction ἦν πειραζόμενος has three adverbial modifiers: the prepositional phrase ἐν τῇ ἐρήμῳ indicating location, the noun phrase τεσσεράκοντα ἡμέρας indicating time, and the prepositional phrase ὑπὸ τοῦ σατανᾶ indicating the agency of the passive participle. As you can see from the translation, trying to capture this in English is awkward. This would be a good test case for comparing various English translations—you will nearly always see "and he was in the wilderness for forty days being tempted by Satan," which somewhat obscures the periphrastic construction but is better English. Notice also the presence of the wild beasts in this verse. This possibly suggests a "restoration of Eden" theme of Jesus's time in the wilderness. The outcome of Jesus's temptation was to begin the process of restoring things to God's original intention for creation. So the overall context here stresses that Jesus was being tempted by Satan, not that Jesus was in the wilderness, which is the subtle shift that occurs in most English translations. Points such as this, however, may not always be rendered in translations and can often be more effectively drawn out in preaching and teaching.

chapter EIGHTEEN

CONTRACT VERBS

You should complete these assignments after you have studied the material for chapter 18 in the textbook and memorized the required vocabulary, paradigms, and principal parts. Once you have completed these assignments to the best of your ability, check your work with the answer key.

For each of the following Greek forms, write out the specified components. Be sure to list all possibilities when applicable. Remember to indicate if a component does not apply for the inflected form by writing any of the following: N/A, n/a, or --.

inflected form	tense	voice	mood	pers	case	num	gender	lexical form	inflected meaning
ἠγάπησας									
δικαιωθέντες									
ἐμαρτύρουν									
καυχᾶσαι									
ζητοῦντες									
ἐγήγερται									
ἐπηρώτησαν									
ᾐτήσατο									
εὑρήκαμεν									
περιεπάτησεν									

TRANSLATION

- For each of the following sentences, double underline each finite verb.
- Put brackets around every [prepositional phrase].
- Single underline each adjective.
- Above each adjective write its function: attributive (ATTR), substantival (SUB), or predicate (PRED).
- Highlight each subordinating conjunction and relative pronoun.
- Put a parenthesis around each (subordinate clause) or (relative clause).
- If applicable, draw an arrow from each relative pronoun to its antecedent.
- Put a square box around every participle.
- Above each participle write its function: adverbial (ADV), attributive (ATTR), or substantival (SUB).
- If applicable, draw an arrow from the participle to the word it modifies.
- Translate the following sentences.

Pop-Up Lexicon

ἀληθῶς	truly
καλῶς	well, commendably, rightly
φρίσσω	I shudder (from fear), I am extremely afraid

1. ἀπεκρίθη αὐτοῖς ὁ Ἰησοῦς, εἶπον ὑμῖν καὶ οὐ πιστεύετε τὰ ἔργα ἃ ἐγὼ ποιῶ ἐν τῷ ὀνόματι τοῦ πατρός μου ταῦτα μαρτυρεῖ περὶ ἐμοῦ.

2. σὺ πιστεύεις ὅτι εἷς ἐστιν ὁ θεός, καλῶς ποιεῖς· καὶ τὰ δαιμόνια πιστεύουσιν καὶ φρίσσουσιν.

3. ὃς δὲ τηρεῖ αὐτοῦ τὸν λόγον, ἀληθῶς ἐν τούτῳ ἡ ἀγάπη τοῦ θεοῦ τετελείωται.

4. τὰ πρόβατα τὰ ἐμὰ τῆς φωνῆς μου ἀκούουσιν, κἀγὼ γινώσκω αὐτὰ καὶ ἀκολουθοῦσίν μοι.

5. καὶ παραχρῆμα ἀνέβλεψεν καὶ ἠκολούθει αὐτῷ δοξάζων τὸν θεόν.

6. καὶ εἰ ἀγαπᾶτε τοὺς ἀγαπῶντας ὑμᾶς, ποία ὑμῖν χάρις ἐστίν; καὶ γὰρ οἱ ἁμαρτωλοὶ τοὺς ἀγαπῶντας αὐτοὺς ἀγαπῶσιν.

7. μακάριος ὁ δοῦλος ἐκεῖνος ὃν ἐλθὼν ὁ κύριος αὐτοῦ εὑρήσει οὕτως ποιοῦντα.

8. πᾶς γὰρ ὁ αἰτῶν λαμβάνει καὶ ὁ ζητῶν εὑρίσκει.

CORRECTION AND ASSESSMENT

Instructions

Once you have completed the parsing and translation exercises to the best of your ability, you may then look at the answer key. On this page, you will find spaces to assess any mistakes you made and to indicate the course of action you took to address the problem.

inflected form or sentence #	assessment	course of action

inflected form or sentence #	assessment	course of action

ANSWER KEY

Parsing

inflected form	tense	voice	mood	pers	case	num	gender	lexical form	inflected meaning
ἠγάπησας	aor	act	ind	2nd	n/a	sg	n/a	ἀγαπάω	you (sg) loved
δικαιωθέντες	aor	pass	ptc	n/a	nom	pl	masc	δικαιόω	ones who were justified
ἐμαρτύρουν	impf	act	ind	1st 3rd	n/a	sg pl	n/a	μαρτυρέω	I was testifying they were testifying
καυχᾶσαι	pres	mid[1]	ind	2nd	n/a	sg	n/a	καυχάομαι	you (sg) boast
ζητοῦντες	pres	act	ptc	n/a	nom	pl	masc	ζητέω	ones who seek
ἐγήγερται	pf	mid pass	ind	3rd	n/a	sg	n/a	ἐγείρω	he/she/it has raised for him-/her-/itself he/she/it has been raised
ἐπηρώτησαν	aor	act	ind	3rd	n/a	pl	n/a	ἐπερωτάω	they asked
ᾐτήσατο	aor	mid	ind	3rd	n/a	sg	n/a	αἰτέω	he/she/it asked for himself/herself/itself
εὑρήκαμεν	pf	act	ind	1st	n/a	pl	n/a	εὑρίσκω	we have found
περιεπάτησεν	aor	act	ind	3rd	n/a	sg	n/a	περιπατέω	he/she/it walked

[1] This verb does not occur in the passive.

Translation

1. ἀπεκρίθη αὐτοῖς ὁ Ἰησοῦς, εἶπον ὑμῖν καὶ οὐ πιστεύετε· τὰ ἔργα (ἃ ἐγὼ ποιῶ [ἐν τῷ ὀνόματι τοῦ πατρός μου]) ταῦτα μαρτυρεῖ [περὶ ἐμοῦ] (John 10:25)

   Jesus answered them, "I spoke to you and you do not believe; the works that I myself am doing in the name of my Father, these things bear witness concerning me."

PRED

2. σὺ πιστεύεις (ὅτι εἷς ἐστιν ὁ θεός), καλῶς ποιεῖς· καὶ τὰ δαιμόνια πιστεύουσιν καὶ φρίσσουσιν (Jas 2:19)

   You yourself believe that God is one, you are doing well; even the demons believe, and they are extremely afraid.

3. (ὃς δὲ τηρεῖ αὐτοῦ τὸν λόγον), ἀληθῶς [ἐν τούτῳ] ἡ ἀγάπη τοῦ θεοῦ τετελείωται (cf. 1 John 2:5)

   And the one who keeps his word, truly, in him the love of God has been perfected.

ATTR

4. τὰ πρόβατα τὰ ἐμὰ τῆς φωνῆς μου ἀκούουσιν, κἀγὼ γινώσκω αὐτὰ καὶ ἀκολουθοῦσίν μοι (John 10:27)

   My sheep hear my voice, and I myself know them and they follow me.

ADV

5. καὶ παραχρῆμα ἀνέβλεψεν καὶ ἠκολούθει αὐτῷ δοξάζων τὸν θεόν (Luke 18:43)

   And immediately he regained [his] sight, and he followed him, glorifying God.

SUB

6. καὶ (εἰ ἀγαπᾶτε τοὺς ἀγαπῶντας ὑμᾶς), ποία ὑμῖν χάρις ἐστίν; καὶ γὰρ οἱ ἁμαρτωλοὶ τοὺς
   SUB
   ἀγαπῶντας αὐτοὺς ἀγαπῶσιν (Luke 6:32)

   And if you love the ones who love you, what kind of benefit is it to you? For even sinners love those who love them.

PRED ADV ATTR

7. μακάριος ὁ δοῦλος ἐκεῖνος (ὃν ἐλθὼν ὁ κύριος αὐτοῦ εὑρήσει οὕτως ποιοῦντα) (Matt 24:46)

   Blessed is that slave whom his lord will find so doing when he comes.

ATTR → SUB SUB

8. πᾶς γὰρ ὁ αἰτῶν λαμβάνει καὶ ὁ ζητῶν εὑρίσκει (Matt 7:8)

   For everyone who asks receives, and the one who seeks finds.

Additional Notes:

- The construction τὰ ἔργα ἃ ἐγὼ ποιῶ ἐν τῷ ὀνόματι τοῦ πατρός μου ταῦτα in sentence 1 (John 10:25) is interesting. This is sometimes described as a "parenthetical nominative" (see Daniel B. Wallace, *Greek Grammar beyond the Basics* [Grand Rapids: Zondervan, 1996], 53–54), where one nominative clause explains or gives further information for the subject. The demonstrative pronoun, ταῦτα, resumes or summarizes the subject phrase and continues the discourse.
- In sentence 3, notice that the demonstrative pronoun τούτῳ functions parallel to a personal pronoun, as is reflected in the translation.
- In sentence 4, μοι is enclitic, which means that it throws its accent back onto the verb: ἀκολουθοῦσίν μοι. You can read more about this if you are curious in appendix 1, "Overview of Greek Accents," found in the grammar.

- In sentence 6, the expression ποία ὑμῖν χάρις ἐστίν is a bit challenging. Ποία is an interrogative pronoun, asking the question "what kind of?" It is modifying χάρις (notice that ποία agrees in case, number, and gender with χάρις), which here refers to something like "favor"—some English translations have "credit" or "benefit." This leads to the rendering "what kind of benefit is it to you?"
- In sentence 7, the subject of the verbless clause is ὁ δοῦλος ἐκεῖνος, and μακάριος is the predicate adjective. Ὁ δοῦλος ἐκεῖνος is further modified by the relative clause.
- In sentence 7, the participle ποιοῦντα is functioning attributively to modify further the relative pronoun, which is why it is in the accusative case. This may seem strange at first, but if you reconstruct the embedded sentence in the relative clause by inserting the antecedent of the relative pronoun, it becomes clear what the participle is modifying:

  TEXT: ὁ δοῦλος ἐκεῖνος ὃν ἐλθὼν ὁ κύριος αὐτοῦ εὑρήσει οὕτως ποιοῦντα.

  REPLACE: relative pronoun with antecedent: τόν δοῦλον ἐκεῖνον ἐλθὼν ὁ κύριος αὐτοῦ εὑρήσει οὕτως ποιοῦντα.

  ADJUST syntax: ἐλθὼν ὁ κύριος αὐτοῦ εὑρήσει τόν δοῦλον ἐκεῖνον οὕτως ποιοῦντα.

  ROUGH TRANSLATION: When he comes, his Lord will find that slave so doing.

chapter NINETEEN

THE FUTURE INDICATIVE AND PARTICIPLE

You should complete these assignments after you have studied the material for chapter 19 in the textbook and memorized the required vocabulary, paradigms, and principal parts. Once you have completed these assignments to the best of your ability, check your work with the answer key.

For each of the following Greek forms, write out the specified components. Be sure to list all possibilities when applicable. Remember to indicate if a component does not apply for the inflected form by writing any of the following: N/A, n/a, or --.

inflected form	tense	voice	mood	pers	case	num	gender	lexical form	inflected meaning
λημψόμεθα									
καθίσει									
ζήσομεν									
ἐρεῖς									
ἀποκτενεῖτε									
εὑρεθησόμεθα									
γενήσεσθε									
συναχθήσονται									
προσκυνήσων									
βλέψετε									

TRANSLATION

- For each of the following sentences, double underline each finite verb.
- Put brackets around every [prepositional phrase].
- Single underline each adjective.
- Above each adjective write its function: attributive (ATTR), substantival (SUB), or predicate (PRED).
- Highlight each subordinating conjunction and relative pronoun.
- Put a parenthesis around each (subordinate clause) or (relative clause).
- If applicable, draw an arrow from each relative pronoun to its antecedent.
- Put a square box around every participle.
- Above each participle write its function: adverbial (ADV), attributive (ATTR), or substantival (SUB).
- If applicable, draw an arrow from the participle to the word it modifies.
- Translate the following sentences.

Pop-Up Lexicon

ἀπιστέω	I refuse to believe, I am unfaithful
κυριεύω	I rule over, I reign
συζάω	I live with, I live together
τελέω	I finish, I complete

1. εἰ δὲ ἀπεθάνομεν σὺν Χριστῷ, πιστεύομεν ὅτι καὶ συζήσομεν αὐτῷ, εἰδότες ὅτι Χριστὸς ἐγερθεὶς ἐκ νεκρῶν οὐκέτι ἀποθνῄσκει, θάνατος αὐτοῦ οὐκέτι κυριεύει.

____

____

2. ἐγὼ ἐβάπτισα ὑμᾶς ὕδατι, αὐτὸς δὲ βαπτίσει ὑμᾶς ἐν πνεύματι ἁγίῳ.

____

3. παραλαβὼν δὲ τοὺς δώδεκα εἶπεν πρὸς αὐτούς, ἰδοὺ ἀναβαίνομεν εἰς Ἰερουσαλήμ, καὶ τελεσθήσεται πάντα τὰ γεγραμμένα διὰ τῶν προφητῶν τῷ υἱῷ τοῦ ἀνθρώπου.

____

____

____

4. καὶ ἐν τούτῳ γνωσόμεθα ὅτι ἐκ τῆς ἀληθείας ἐσμέν, καὶ ἔμπροσθεν αὐτοῦ πείσομεν τὴν καρδίαν ἡμῶν.

5. καὶ λέγει αὐτῷ, ἀμὴν ἀμὴν λέγω ὑμῖν, ὄψεσθε τὸν οὐρανὸν ἀνεῳγότα καὶ τοὺς ἀγγέλους τοῦ θεοῦ ἀναβαίνοντας καὶ καταβαίνοντας ἐπὶ τὸν υἱὸν τοῦ ἀνθρώπου.

6. τέξεται δὲ υἱόν, καὶ καλέσεις τὸ ὄνομα αὐτοῦ Ἰησοῦν· αὐτὸς γὰρ σώσει τὸν λαὸν αὐτοῦ ἀπὸ τῶν ἁμαρτιῶν αὐτῶν.

7. ὁ πιστεύσας καὶ βαπτισθεὶς σωθήσεται, ὁ δὲ ἀπιστήσας κατακριθήσεται.

CORRECTION AND ASSESSMENT

Instructions

Once you have completed the parsing and translation exercises to the best of your ability, you may then look at the answer key. On this page, you will find spaces to assess any mistakes you made and to indicate the course of action you took to address the problem.

inflected form or sentence #	assessment	course of action

inflected form or sentence #	assessment	course of action

ANSWER KEY

Parsing

inflected form	tense	voice	mood	pers	case	num	gender	lexical form	inflected meaning
λημψόμεθα	fut	mid	ind	1st	n/a	pl	n/a	λαμβάνω	we will receive
καθίσει	fut	act	ind	3rd	n/a	sg	n/a	καθίζω	he/she/it will sit
ζήσομεν	fut	act	ind	1st	n/a	pl	n/a	ζάω	we will live
ἐρεῖς	fut	act	ind	2nd	n/a	sg	n/a	λέγω	you (sg) will say
ἀποκτενεῖτε	fut	act	ind	2nd	n/a	pl	n/a	ἀποκτείνω	you (pl) will die
εὑρεθησόμεθα	fut	pass	ind	1st	n/a	pl	n/a	εὑρίσκω	we will be found
γενήσεσθε	fut	mid	ind	2nd	n/a	pl	n/a	γίνομαι	you will become
συναχθήσονται	fut	pass	ind	3rd	n/a	pl	n/a	συνάγω	they will be gathered they will gather[1]
προσκυνήσων	fut	act	ptc	n/a	nom	sg	masc	προσκυνέω	one (masc) who will worship
βλέψετε	fut	act	ind	2nd	n/a	pl	n/a	βλέπω	you (pl) will see

[1] Recall from chapter 14 that this verb usually has an intransitive, active sense, so this second translation is far more common.

Translation

1. (εἰ δὲ ἀπεθάνομεν [σὺν Χριστῷ]), πιστεύομεν (ὅτι καὶ συζήσομεν αὐτῷ, εἰδότες (ὅτι Χριστὸς ἐγερθεὶς [ἐκ νεκρῶν] οὐκέτι ἀποθνῄσκει, θάνατος αὐτοῦ οὐκέτι κυριεύει)) (Rom 6:8–9)

   ADV ADV

   And if we died with Christ, we believe that we will also live together with him, knowing that because Christ has been raised from the dead, he is no longer dead; death no longer reigns over him.

2. ἐγὼ ἐβάπτισα ὑμᾶς ὕδατι, αὐτὸς δὲ βαπτίσει ὑμᾶς [ἐν πνεύματι ἁγίῳ] (Mark 1:8)

I myself baptized you with water, but he himself will baptize you with the Holy Spirit.

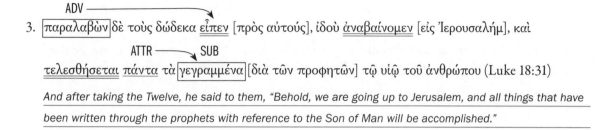

ADV →

3. παραλαβὼν δὲ τοὺς δώδεκα εἶπεν [πρὸς αὐτούς], ἰδοὺ ἀναβαίνομεν [εἰς Ἰερουσαλήμ], καὶ

ATTR → SUB

τελεσθήσεται πάντα τὰ γεγραμμένα [διὰ τῶν προφητῶν] τῷ υἱῷ τοῦ ἀνθρώπου (Luke 18:31)

And after taking the Twelve, he said to them, "Behold, we are going up to Jerusalem, and all things that have been written through the prophets with reference to the Son of Man will be accomplished."

4. καὶ [ἐν τούτῳ] γνωσόμεθα (ὅτι [ἐκ τῆς ἀληθείας] ἐσμέν), καὶ [ἔμπροσθεν αὐτοῦ] πείσομεν τὴν καρδίαν ἡμῶν (1 John 3:19)

And by this we will know that we are of the truth, and we will reassure our heart before him.

← ATTR

5. καὶ λέγει αὐτῷ, ἀμὴν ἀμὴν λέγω ὑμῖν, ὄψεσθε τὸν οὐρανὸν ἀνεῳγότα καὶ τοὺς ἀγγέλους τοῦ

ATTR ATTR →

θεοῦ ἀναβαίνοντας καὶ καταβαίνοντας [ἐπὶ τὸν υἱὸν τοῦ ἀνθρώπου] (John 1:51)

And he says to him, "Truly truly I say to you, you will see heaven opening and the angels of God ascending and descending upon the Son of Man."

6. τέξεται δὲ υἱόν, καὶ καλέσεις τὸ ὄνομα αὐτοῦ Ἰησοῦν· αὐτὸς γὰρ σώσει τὸν λαὸν αὐτοῦ [ἀπὸ τῶν ἁμαρτιῶν αὐτῶν] (Matt 1:21)

And she will bear a son, and you will call his name Jesus; for he himself will save his people from their sins.

SUB SUB SUB

7. ὁ πιστεύσας καὶ βαπτισθεὶς σωθήσεται, ὁ δὲ ἀπιστήσας κατακριθήσεται (Mark 16:16)

The one who believes and is baptized will be saved, but the one who does not believe will be condemned.

Additional Notes:

- In sentence 1, the subordinating conjunction εἰ introduces the protasis of a first-class conditional in Romans 6:8–9. Both ὅτι clauses indicate the content of the verb form that immediately precedes the ὅτι.
- In sentence 1, both adverbial participles, εἰδότες and ἐγερθείς, are functioning causally. They both could be rendered with either "because" or "since" to indicate this function in English. The translation here is a more natural use of English. Notice that a causal participle is often translated as a dependent clause in English with a finite verb (e.g., "because Christ has been raised from the dead").
- Also in sentence 1, although you may have rendered οὐκέτι ἀποθνῄσκει as "he is no longer dying," it is clear from the overall context that "he is no longer dead" is intended. Context also helps to understand the next clause: θάνατος αὐτοῦ οὐκέτι κυριεύει. "His death no longer reigns" makes no sense theologically. If you look up κυριεύω in a lexicon, you will find that it takes its object in the genitive case,

as reflected in the translation. The somewhat unusual placement of αὐτοῦ (called "fronting") could indicate emphasis.

- In sentence 2 we find a classic example of the emphatic use of personal pronouns in the nominative case. Notice also how this usage amplifies the contrast that John the Baptist makes between his own ministry and that of Jesus.
- In sentence 2, the preposition ἐν could also be translated "in." As noted, prepositions can be theologically significant. You can compare various English translations to see how this preposition is translated. A good commentary should discuss the theological implications of the various translation options.
- Sentence 3 gives a nice example of the dative case indicating reference: τῷ υἱῷ τοῦ ἀνθρώπου means "with reference to the Son of Man."
- The ὅτι clause in sentence 4 indicates the content of the verb γνωσόμεθα.
- The glosses that you learned for πείθω were "I persuade, I convince, I satisfy." But as you can see, those glosses don't really work in sentence 4. This verb has a fairly wide semantic range. Many English translations have "reassure," which we have used here.
- In sentence 4, the prepositional phrase ἐν τούτῳ could also be translated "by this."
- Note the use of the plural personal pronoun (ἡμῶν) with a singular noun (καρδίαν) in sentence 4. This is fairly common.
- Sentence 7 is Mark 16:16, which is part of the disputed longer ending of Mark's Gospel. Many scholars believe that the Gospel ends at 16:8 and that this section was added later, apparently in an attempt to smooth out the abrupt ending at verse 8. There is good reason to accept verse 8 as the end of the Gospel, however. The women's fear is consistent with the overall theme of the disciples' failure and the implication that true disciples should move beyond the doubt and fear depicted by Jesus's disciples. Clearly this is what the women at the tomb in fact did—otherwise we would not have their vital testimony! Additionally, the longer ending of Mark's Gospel contains some theological ideas that are not present in the rest of the Gospel, such as the implication that baptism itself is salvific in Mark 16:16. You can read more about this in any standard critical commentary on Mark's Gospel.

chapter TWENTY

TEXT FOR INTEGRATION

You can make a copy of this text to accompany your work on the integration exercises for chapter 20 in the textbook.

Pop-Up Lexicon

βαπτιστής, -οῦ, ὁ	Baptist (of John)
Ἠλίας, -ου, ὁ	Elijah
Καισάρεια, -ας, ἡ	Caesarea
λῃστής, οῦ, ὁ	robber
προσευχή, -ῆς, ἡ	prayer, place of prayer
Φίλιππος, -ου, ὁ	Philip

Hint: If you don't recognize a verb form, be sure to consult appendix 14, "Principal Parts Chart," in the textbook.

1. Καὶ ἐξῆλθεν ὁ Ἰησοῦς καὶ οἱ μαθηταὶ αὐτοῦ εἰς τὰς κώμας Καισαρείας τῆς Φιλίππου·

2. καὶ ἐν τῇ ὁδῷ ἐπηρώτα τοὺς μαθητὰς αὐτοῦ λέγων αὐτοῖς·

3. τί περὶ ἐμοῦ λέγουσιν οἱ ἄνθρωποι;

4. οἱ δὲ εἶπαν αὐτῷ

5. τινες λέγουσιν ὅτι σὺ εἶ Ἰωάννης ὁ βαπτιστής, καὶ τινες Ἠλίας,

6. τινες δὲ ὅτι εἷς τῶν προφητῶν.

7. καὶ αὐτὸς ἐπηρώτα αὐτούς· ὑμεῖς δὲ τί περὶ ἐμοῦ λέγετε;

8. ἀποκριθεὶς ὁ Πέτρος λέγει αὐτῷ· σὺ εἶ ὁ χριστός.

9. Τότε ἐδίδασκεν τοὺς μαθητὰς αὐτοῦ καὶ ἔλεγεν αὐτοῖς ὅτι

10. ὁ υἱὸς τοῦ ἀνθρώπου ἀπεκτάνθη ἐν χειρὶν ἀνθρώπων,

11. καὶ ἀποκτανθεὶς μετὰ τρεῖς ἡμέρας ἐγερθήσεται.

12. Καὶ ἔρχονται εἰς Ἱεροσόλυμα. Καὶ εἰσελθὼν εἰς τὸ ἱερὸν ἐκέβαλεν τοὺς πωλοῦντας

13. καὶ τοὺς ἀγοράζοντας ἐν τῷ ἱερῷ. καὶ ἐδίδασκεν καὶ ἔλεγεν αὐτοῖς,

14. οὐ γέγραπται ὅτι ὁ οἶκός μου οἶκος προσευχῆς κληθήσεται πᾶσιν τοῖς ἔθνεσιν;

15. ὑμεῖς δὲ πεποιήκατε αὐτὸν οἶκον λῃστῶν.

16. Καὶ ἤκουσαν οἱ ἀρχιερεῖς καὶ οἱ γραμματεῖς καὶ ἐζήτουν πῶς αὐτὸν ἀποκτενοῦσιν·

17. ἐφοβοῦντο γὰρ αὐτόν, πᾶς γὰρ ὁ ὄχλος ἐθαυμάζοντο ἐπὶ τῇ διδαχῇ αὐτοῦ.

chapter TWENTY-ONE

THE SUBJUNCTIVE: *Forms and Functions*

You should complete these assignments after you have studied the material for chapter 21 in the textbook and memorized the required vocabulary, paradigms, and principal parts. Once you have completed these assignments to the best of your ability, check your work with the answer key.

For each of the following Greek forms, write out the specified components. Be sure to list all possibilities when applicable. Remember to indicate if a component does not apply for the inflected form by writing any of the following: N/A, n/a, or --.

inflected form	tense	voice	mood	pers	case	num	gender	lexical form	inflected meaning
διδάσκῃ									
λάβωμεν									
ἐγερθῇ									
πίω									
ἄγωμεν									
εἴπῃς									
βάλω									
ἀγαπᾷ									
πέσωσιν									
ἔλθητε									

TRANSLATION

- For each of the following sentences, double underline each finite verb.
- Put brackets around every [prepositional phrase].
- Single underline each adjective.
- Above each adjective write its function: attributive (ATTR), substantival (SUB), or predicate (PRED).
- Highlight each subordinating conjunction and relative pronoun.
- Put a parenthesis around each (subordinate clause) or (relative clause).
- If applicable, draw an arrow from each relative pronoun to its antecedent.
- Put a square box around every participle.
- Above each participle write its function: adverbial (ADV), attributive (ATTR), or substantival (SUB).
- If applicable, draw an arrow from the participle to the word it modifies.
- Translate the following sentences.

Pop-Up Lexicon

ἐνδύω	I clothe, I wear
λίμνη, -ης, ἡ	lake
μισθός, -οῦ, ὁ	pay, wages, reward
πλουτέω	I am rich, I become rich, I am generous
πτωχεία, -ας, ἡ	poverty
πτωχεύω	I am poor, I become poor

1. καὶ πᾶς ὁ ζῶν καὶ πιστεύων εἰς ἐμὲ οὐ μὴ ἀποθάνῃ εἰς τὸν αἰῶνα. πιστεύεις τοῦτο;

____

____

2. ἐὰν γὰρ ἀγαπήσητε τοὺς ἀγαπῶντας ὑμᾶς, τίνα μισθὸν ἔχετε; οὐχὶ καὶ οἱ τελῶναι τὸ αὐτὸ ποιοῦσιν;

____

____

3. ἐν τούτῳ γινώσκομεν ὅτι ἀγαπῶμεν τὰ τέκνα τοῦ θεοῦ, ὅταν τὸν θεὸν ἀγαπῶμεν καὶ τὰς ἐντολὰς αὐτοῦ ποιῶμεν.

___

___

4. ἐγένετο δὲ ἐν μιᾷ τῶν ἡμερῶν καὶ αὐτὸς ἐνέβη εἰς πλοῖον καὶ οἱ μαθηταὶ αὐτοῦ καὶ εἶπεν πρὸς αὐτούς, διέλθωμεν εἰς τὸ πέραν τῆς λίμνης, καὶ ἀνήχθησαν.

___

___

5. καὶ εἶπεν ὁ Ἰησοῦς, εἰς κρίμα ἐγὼ εἰς τὸν κόσμον τοῦτον ἦλθον, ἵνα οἱ μὴ βλέποντες βλέπωσιν καὶ οἱ βλέποντες τυφλοὶ γένωνται.

___

___

6. διὰ τοῦτο λέγω ὑμῖν, μὴ μεριμνᾶτε τῇ ψυχῇ ὑμῶν τί φάγητε ἢ τί πίητε, μηδὲ τῷ σώματι ὑμῶν τί ἐνδύσησθε.

___

___

7. λέγει αὐτῷ Πέτρος, οὐ μὴ νίψῃς μου τοὺς πόδας εἰς τὸν αἰῶνα. ἀπεκρίθη Ἰησοῦς αὐτῷ, ἐὰν μὴ νίψω σε, οὐκ ἔχεις μέρος μετʼ ἐμοῦ.

___

___

8. ἐὰν εἰδῆτε ὅτι δίκαιός ἐστιν, γινώσκετε ὅτι καὶ πᾶς ὁ ποιῶν τὴν δικαιοσύνην ἐξ αὐτοῦ γεγέννηται.

9. γινώσκετε γὰρ τὴν χάριν τοῦ κυρίου ἡμῶν Ἰησοῦ Χριστοῦ, ὅτι δι' ὑμᾶς ἐπτώχευσεν πλούσιος ὤν, ἵνα ὑμεῖς τῇ ἐκείνου πτωχείᾳ πλουτήσητε.

CORRECTION AND ASSESSMENT

Instructions

Once you have completed the parsing and translation exercises to the best of your ability, you may then look at the answer key. On this page, you will find spaces to assess any mistakes you made and to indicate the course of action you took to address the problem.

inflected form or sentence #	assessment	course of action

ANSWER KEY

Parsing

inflected form	tense	voice	mood	pers	case	num	gender	lexical form	inflected meaning
διδάσκῃ	pres	mid pass act mid pass	ind ind subj subj subj	2nd 2nd 3rd 2nd 2nd	n/a	sg sg sg sg sg	n/a	διδάσκω	you (sg) teach for yourself you (sg) are taught he/she/it may teach you (sg) may teach for yourself you (sg) may be taught
λάβωμεν	aor	act	subj	1st	n/a	pl	n/a	λαμβάνω	we might receive
ἐγερθῇ	aor	pass	subj	3rd	n/a	sg	n/a	ἐγείρω	he/she/it might be raised
πίω	aor	act	subj	1st	n/a	sg	n/a	πίνω	I might drink
ἄγωμεν	pres	act	subj	1st	n/a	pl	n/a	ἄγω	we may go
εἴπῃς	aor	act	subj	2nd	n/a	sg	n/a	λέγω	you (sg) might say
βάλω	aor	act	subj	1st	n/a	sg	n/a	βάλλω	I might throw
ἀγαπᾷ	pres	act mid pass act mid pass	ind ind ind subj subj subj	3rd 2nd 2nd 3rd 2nd 2nd	n/a	sg sg sg sg sg sg	n/a	ἀγαπάω	he/she/it loves you (sg) love for yourself you (sg) are loved he/she/it may love you (sg) may love for yourself you (sg) may be loved
πέσωσιν	aor	act	subj	3rd	n/a	pl	n/a	πίπτω	they might fall
ἔλθητε	aor	act	subj	2nd	n/a	pl	n/a	ἔρχομαι	you (pl) might go

Translation

SUB SUB emphatic denial

1. καὶ πᾶς ὁ ζῶν καὶ πιστεύων [εἰς ἐμὲ] οὐ μὴ ἀποθάνῃ [εἰς τὸν αἰῶνα]. πιστεύεις τοῦτο; (John 11:26)

   And everyone who lives and believes in me will surely not die forever. Do you believe this?

SUB

2. (ἐὰν γὰρ ἀγαπήσητε τοὺς ἀγαπῶντας ὑμᾶς), τίνα μισθὸν ἔχετε; οὐχὶ καὶ οἱ τελῶναι τὸ αὐτὸ ποιοῦσιν; (Matt 5:46)

   For if you love those who love you, what reward do you have? Don't even the tax collectors do the same?

3. [ἐν τούτῳ] γινώσκομεν (ὅτι ἀγαπῶμεν τὰ τέκνα τοῦ θεοῦ), (ὅταν τὸν θεὸν ἀγαπῶμεν καὶ τὰς ἐντολὰς αὐτοῦ ποιῶμεν) (1 John 5:2)

   By this we know that we love the children of God, when we love God and we keep his commandments.

4. ἐγένετο δὲ [ἐν μιᾷ τῶν ἡμερῶν] καὶ αὐτὸς ἐνέβη [εἰς πλοῖον] καὶ οἱ μαθηταὶ αὐτοῦ καὶ εἶπεν

hortatory
[πρὸς αὐτούς], διέλθωμεν [εἰς τὸ πέραν τῆς λίμνης], καὶ ἀνήχθησαν (Luke 8:22)

And it happened on one of the days, and he himself got into a boat with his disciples, and he said to them, "Let us go over to the other side of the lake," and they set sail.

SUB
5. καὶ εἶπεν ὁ Ἰησοῦς, [εἰς κρίμα] ἐγὼ [εἰς τὸν κόσμον τοῦτον] ἦλθον, (ἵνα οἱ μὴ βλέποντες

SUB PRED
βλέπωσιν καὶ οἱ βλέποντες τυφλοὶ γένωνται) (John 9:39)

And Jesus said, "For judgment I myself came into this world, in order that those who do not see may see and those who see may become blind."

prohibition deliberative deliberative
6. [διὰ τοῦτο] λέγω ὑμῖν, μὴ μεριμνᾶτε τῇ ψυχῇ ὑμῶν τί φάγητε ἢ τί πίητε, μηδὲ τῷ σώματι ὑμῶν

deliberative
τί ἐνδύσησθε (Matt 6:25)

Therefore I say to you, "Do not worry about your life, what you will eat or what you will drink, nor for your body, what you will wear."

emphatic denial
7. λέγει αὐτῷ Πέτρος, οὐ μὴ νίψῃς μου τοὺς πόδας [εἰς τὸν αἰῶνα]. ἀπεκρίθη Ἰησοῦς αὐτῷ, (ἐὰν μὴ νίψω σε), οὐκ ἔχεις μέρος [μετ᾽ ἐμοῦ] (John 13:8)

Peter said to him, "You will certainly not wash my feet ever." Jesus answered him, "Unless I wash you, you have no part with me."

PRED ATTR SUB
8. (ἐὰν εἰδῆτε (ὅτι δίκαιός ἐστιν)), γινώσκετε (ὅτι καὶ πᾶς ὁ ποιῶν τὴν δικαιοσύνην [ἐξ αὐτοῦ] γεγέννηται) (1 John 2:29)

If you know that he is righteous, you know that also everyone who practices righteousness has been born from him.

PRED
9. γινώσκετε γὰρ τὴν χάριν τοῦ κυρίου ἡμῶν Ἰησοῦ Χριστοῦ, (ὅτι [δι᾽ ὑμᾶς] ἐπτώχευσεν πλούσιος

ADV
ὤν, (ἵνα ὑμεῖς τῇ ἐκείνου πτωχείᾳ πλουτήσητε)) (2 Cor 8:9)

For you know the grace of our Lord Jesus Christ, that on account of you he became poor though he was rich, so that you yourselves may be rich through his poverty.

Additional Notes:

- Notice the example of emphatic negation in sentence 1. There are numerous ways to render this in English. This would be a good time to compare English translations.
- Sentence 2 is a good example of a third-class conditional. Notice that there is no assumption that is made for the sake the argument as is the case with first- and second-class conditionals. Also notice that an English modal, such as "would" or "might," is unnecessary when translating a third-class conditional; the "if" is sufficient for rendering this hypothetical condition.
- In sentence 3, notice that the ὅτι clause is functioning to indicate the content of γινώσκομεν.
- In sentence 3, it is unnecessary to translate ὅταν "whenever"; in fact, this gives the wrong connotation in English. The ὅταν clause is functioning epexegetically to explain the circumstances that indicate how and when the readers know their love for other believers. This is a good example of needing to pay attention to the overall context when translating Greek constructions.
- In sentence 4, note the expression ἐγένετο δέ. It is very common in Luke and signals a new event or pericope. It is not uncommon for English translations to leave this expression untranslated; for example, some translations of Luke 8:22 simply have, "One day, Jesus . . ."
- In sentence 4, the subject of the verb ἐνέβη is clearly Jesus, but the disciples also got into the boat. Because οἱ μαθηταί is in the nominative, it is also the subject of the verb. In English, when there is a compound subject, the verb is usually plural. Not so in Greek! So we have translated καὶ οἱ μαθηταὶ αὐτοῦ as "with his disciples," but you could also translate this clause as follows: "He himself and his disciples got into a boat . . ."
- Notice the hortatory subjunctive in sentence 4. There are several clear contextual clues that this is a hortatory subjunctive. First, there is no subordinating conjunction such as ἵνα or ἐάν before the subjunctive. Next, notice the switch from the third-person εἶπεν to the first-person διέλθωμεν and back to the third-person ἀνήχθησαν. This is a good indication of direct discourse, where hortatory subjunctives often occur.
- Sentence 6 offers three clear examples of deliberative subjunctives. Notice also the good example of a prohibition. You may have translated τῇ ψυχῇ ὑμῶν as "for your life," and that would be an acceptable translation. It reflects more natural English.
- Sentence 7 is a good example of a historical present used in a narrative to signal direct discourse. The translation reflects English convention, which would not use a present-tense verb in a narrative context.
- The clause, οὐ μὴ νίψῃς μου τοὺς πόδας εἰς τὸν αἰῶνα, in sentence 7 could also be translated as follows: "Surely you will never wash my feet!"
- Both ὅτι clauses in sentence 8 are functioning to indicate the content of the preceding verb.
- The ὅτι clause in sentence 9 is functioning epexegetically to further explain the grace of our Lord Jesus Christ. The participle ὤν is an adverbial concessive participle used to indicate something that is true despite the finite verb that it modifies; namely, although Christ is rich (πλούσιος ὤν) he became poor (ἐπτώχευσεν) for our sake.

chapter TWENTY-TWO

THE IMPERATIVE:

Forms and Functions; More Pronouns

You should complete these assignments after you have studied the material for chapter 22 in the textbook and memorized the required vocabulary, paradigms, and principal parts. Once you have completed these assignments to the best of your ability, check your work with the answer key.

For each of the following Greek forms, write out the specified components. Be sure to list all possibilities when applicable. Remember to indicate if a component does not apply for the inflected form by writing any of the following: N/A, n/a, or --.

inflected form	tense	voice	mood	pers	case	num	gender	lexical form	inflected meaning
ἐσθίετε									
ἀνάβα									
βλήθητι									
πίστευσον									
ἔστωσαν									
ποιήσατε									
σωσάτω									
γενηθήτω									
κήρυξον									
κάλει									

TRANSLATION

- For each of the following sentences, double underline each finite verb.
- Put brackets around every [prepositional phrase].
- Single underline each adjective.
- Above each adjective write its function: attributive (ATTR), substantival (SUB), or predicate (PRED).
- Highlight each subordinating conjunction and relative pronoun.
- Put a parenthesis around each (subordinate clause) or (relative clause).
- If applicable, draw an arrow from each relative pronoun to its antecedent.
- Put a square box around every participle.
- Above each participle write its function: adverbial (ADV), attributive (ATTR), or substantival (SUB).
- If applicable, draw an arrow from the participle to the word it modifies.
- Translate the following sentences.

Pop-Up Lexicon

ἐμφανίζω	I make known, I reveal
μετεωρίζομαι	I worry, I am upset
συναντάω	I meet, I happen
χρήζω	I need, I have need of

1. μὴ ταρασσέσθω ὑμῶν ἡ καρδία· πιστεύετε εἰς τὸν θεὸν καὶ εἰς ἐμὲ πιστεύετε.

2. οὐ πιστεύεις ὅτι ἐγὼ ἐν τῷ πατρὶ καὶ ὁ πατὴρ ἐν ἐμοί ἐστιν; τὰ ῥήματα ἃ ἐγὼ λέγω ὑμῖν ἀπ' ἐμαυτοῦ οὐ λαλῶ, ὁ δὲ πατὴρ ἐν ἐμοὶ μένων ποιεῖ τὰ ἔργα αὐτοῦ.

3. πάντοτε γὰρ τοὺς πτωχοὺς ἔχετε μεθ' ἑαυτῶν, ἐμὲ δὲ οὐ πάντοτε ἔχετε.

4. οὐ γὰρ ἑαυτοὺς κηρύσσομεν ἀλλὰ Ἰησοῦν Χριστὸν κύριον, ἑαυτοὺς δὲ δούλους ὑμῶν διὰ Ἰησοῦν.

5. καὶ ὑμεῖς μὴ ζητεῖτε τί φάγητε καὶ τί πίητε καὶ μὴ μετεωρίζεσθε· ταῦτα γὰρ πάντα τὰ ἔθνη τοῦ κόσμου ἐπιζητοῦσιν, ὑμῶν δὲ ὁ πατὴρ οἶδεν ὅτι χρῄζετε τούτων.

6. ὁ ἔχων ὦτα ἀκουέτω.

7. ὁ ἔχων τὰς ἐντολάς μου καὶ τηρῶν αὐτὰς ἐκεῖνός ἐστιν ὁ ἀγαπῶν με· ὁ δὲ ἀγαπῶν με ἀγαπηθήσεται ὑπὸ τοῦ πατρός μου, κἀγὼ ἀγαπήσω αὐτὸν καὶ ἐμφανίσω αὐτῷ ἐμαυτόν.

8. καὶ ἐφοβήθησαν φόβον μέγαν καὶ ἔλεγον πρὸς ἀλλήλους, τίς ἄρα οὗτός ἐστιν ὅτι καὶ ὁ ἄνεμος καὶ ἡ θάλασσα ὑπακούει αὐτῷ;

9. ὁ δὲ εἶπεν αὐτοῖς, ἰδοὺ εἰσελθόντων ὑμῶν εἰς τὴν πόλιν συναντήσει ὑμῖν ἄνθρωπος . . . ἀκολουθήσατε αὐτῷ εἰς τὴν οἰκίαν εἰς ἣν εἰσπορεύεται.

CORRECTION AND ASSESSMENT

Instructions

Once you have completed the parsing and translation exercises to the best of your ability, you may then look at the answer key. On this page, you will find spaces to assess any mistakes you made and to indicate the course of action you took to address the problem.

inflected form or sentence #	assessment	course of action

ANSWER KEY

Parsing

inflected form	tense	voice	mood	pers	case	num	gender	lexical form	inflected meaning
ἐσθίετε	pres	act act	ind impv	2nd	n/a	pl	n/a	ἐσθίω	you (pl) eat (you pl) eat!
ἀνάβα	aor	act	impv	2nd	n/a	sg	n/a	ἀναβαίνω	(you sg) go up!
βλήθητι	aor	pass	impv	2nd	n/a	sg	n/a	βάλλω	(you sg) be thrown!
πίστευσον	aor	act	impv	2nd	n/a	sg	n/a	πιστεύω	(you sg) believe!
ἔστωσαν	pres	n/a	impv	3rd	n/a	pl	n/a	εἰμί	let them be!
ποιήσατε	aor	act	impv	2nd	n/a	pl	n/a	ποιέω	(you pl) do!
σωσάτω	aor	act	impv	3rd	n/a	sg	n/a	σῴζω	let him/her/it save!

inflected form	tense	voice	mood	pers	case	num	gender	lexical form	inflected meaning
γενηθήτω	aor	pass	impv	3rd	n/a	sg	n/a	γίνομαι	let him/her/it become!
κήρυξον	aor	act	impv	2nd	n/a	sg	n/a	κηρύσσω	(you sg) preach!
κάλει	pres	act	impv	2nd	n/a	sg	n/a	καλέω	(you sg) call!

Additional Notes:

- If you thought that κάλει could also have been a present active indicative, you were very close! The indicative form is καλεῖ, with the circumflex indicating vowel contraction.

Translation

1. μὴ ταρασσέσθω ὑμῶν ἡ καρδία· πιστεύετε [εἰς τὸν θεὸν] καὶ [εἰς ἐμὲ] πιστεύετε (John 14:1)

   Let not your hearts be troubled; believe in God and believe in me.

2. οὐ πιστεύεις (ὅτι ἐγὼ [ἐν τῷ πατρὶ] καὶ ὁ πατὴρ [ἐν ἐμοί] ἐστιν); τὰ ῥήματα (ἃ ἐγὼ λέγω ὑμῖν)
   ATTR
   [ἀπ' ἐμαυτοῦ] οὐ λαλῶ, ὁ δὲ πατὴρ [ἐν ἐμοὶ] μένων ποιεῖ τὰ ἔργα αὐτοῦ (John 14:10)

   Do you not believe that I am in the Father and the Father is in me? The words that I myself am saying to you I do not speak from myself, but the Father who remains in me does his works.

3. SUB
   πάντοτε γὰρ τοὺς πτωχοὺς ἔχετε [μεθ' ἑαυτῶν], ἐμὲ δὲ οὐ πάντοτε ἔχετε (Matt 26:11)

   For you always have the poor with you, but you do not always have me.

4. οὐ γὰρ ἑαυτοὺς κηρύσσομεν ἀλλὰ Ἰησοῦν Χριστὸν κύριον, ἑαυτοὺς δὲ δούλους ὑμῶν [διὰ Ἰησοῦν] (2 Cor 4:5)

   For we did not preach ourselves, but [we preach] Jesus Christ the Lord, and ourselves as your slaves because of Jesus.

5. ATTR
   καὶ ὑμεῖς μὴ ζητεῖτε τί φάγητε καὶ τί πίητε καὶ μὴ μετεωρίζεσθε· ταῦτα γὰρ πάντα τὰ ἔθνη τοῦ κόσμου ἐπιζητοῦσιν, ὑμῶν δὲ ὁ πατὴρ οἶδεν (ὅτι χρῄζετε τούτων) (Luke 12:29–30)

   And (you) do not seek what you should eat and what you should drink and do not be anxious; for the nations of the world seek after all these things, but your Father knows that you have need of these things.

6. SUB
   ὁ ἔχων ὦτα ἀκουέτω (Matt 13:9)

   The one who has ears, let him hear.

SUB SUB SUB SUB
7. ὁ ἔχων τὰς ἐντολάς μου καὶ τηρῶν αὐτὰς ἐκεῖνός ἐστιν ὁ ἀγαπῶν με· ὁ δὲ ἀγαπῶν με ἀγαπηθήσεται [ὑπὸ τοῦ πατρός μου], κἀγὼ ἀγαπήσω αὐτὸν καὶ ἐμφανίσω αὐτῷ ἐμαυτόν (John 14:21)

The one who has my commandments and keeps them, that one is the one who loves me; and the one who loves me will be loved by my Father, and I myself will love him and will reveal myself to him.

ATTR
8. καὶ ἐφοβήθησαν φόβον μέγαν καὶ ἔλεγον [πρὸς ἀλλήλους], τίς ἄρα οὗτός ἐστιν (ὅτι καὶ ὁ ἄνεμος καὶ ἡ θάλασσα ὑπακούει αὐτῷ); (Mark 4:41)

And they feared a great fear and they were saying to one another, "Who then is this one, that even the wind and the sea obey him?"

ADV; GA
9. ὁ δὲ εἶπεν αὐτοῖς, ἰδοὺ εἰσελθόντων ὑμῶν [εἰς τὴν πόλιν] συναντήσει ὑμῖν ἄνθρωπος . . . ἀκολουθήσατε αὐτῷ [εἰς τὴν οἰκίαν] ([εἰς ἣν] εἰσπορεύεται) (Luke 22:10)

And he said to them, "Look, when you enter the city, a man will meet you . . . follow him into the house into which he enters."

Additional Notes:

- In sentence 1, notice that ὑμῶν is plural but ἡ καρδία is singular. This is common, especially in John's writings. The fact that this discourse is addressed to more than one person, based on the second-person plural imperatives that follow, indicates that this opening imperative is also addressed to all of Jesus's disciples. This is reflected in the translation "your heart*s*."
- In sentence 1, μὴ ταρασσέσθω is a good example of a third-person imperative, or more specifically, a prohibition. Many English translations have, "Do no let your hearts be troubled," which reflects English usage better. The translation here better reflects the third-person imperative in the Greek.
- The ὅτι clause in sentence 2 is functioning to indicate the content of the verb πιστεύεις.
- The antecedent for ἅ in sentence 2 is τὰ ῥήματα. The relative pronoun is in the accusative case because it is functioning as the direct object of λέγω.
- Although the form ἔχετε could be indicative or imperative, the overall context of Matthew 26:11 in sentence 3 makes it clear that both occurrences of this verb are indicatives. This also explains the translation for μεθ' ἑαυτῶν as "with you"; even though ἑαυτῶν is a third-person reflexive pronoun, it can function to indicate a first- or second-person referent as well. This parallels the emphatic use of αὐτός (third-person personal pronoun) in the nominative case with first- and second-person subjects.
- Sentence 4 is good example of how reflexive pronouns are used. It is also a good example of ellipsis—where verbs or phrases are not explicitly repeated, but they are clearly implied. This is indicated in the translation with square brackets.
- Sentence 5 contains good examples of deliberative subjunctives. The emphatic use of the personal pronoun ὑμεῖς is difficult to render in translation; we have put it in a parenthesis, but most translations simply leave it untranslated. The collocation ταῦτα γὰρ πάντα τὰ ἔθνη poses an interesting interpretive challenge. Once the postpositive γάρ is "removed," it is unclear whether πάντα is modifying ταῦτα

or τὰ ἔθνη; either option is viable syntactically. In the overall context, however, the preceding series of imperatives appear to be viewed together as "things." Moreover, there is no emphasis on the nations in the pericope, so it seems more likely that πάντα goes with ταῦτα and not τὰ ἔθνη. This is a good time to compare various English translations—you'll see that not all translation committees agree with our assessment!

- Sentence 6 offers a good example of a third-person imperative.
- The use of ἐκεῖνος in sentence 7 is interesting. The actual form ἐκεῖνός has two accents because the ἐστιν immediately following is an enclitic, meaning that it "throws" its accent back on the preceding word. Additionally, it is a good example of the demonstrative pronoun functioning parallel to a personal pronoun; the translation "that one" is an overtranslation; many English translations have "the one" or "he." It is also interesting because the demonstrative is unnecessary syntactically. The subject phrase, ὁ ἔχων τὰς ἐντολάς μου καὶ τηρῶν αὐτάς, is a bit long, however, so here ἐκεῖνος functions to "resume" the sentence. Technically, ὁ ἔχων τὰς ἐντολάς μου καὶ τηρῶν αὐτάς is called a "hanging nominative," because it is syntactically hanging off by itself.
- Notice also the future indicative in sentence 7. It is hard to miss the form of the future passive indicative!
- There are several elements in sentence 8 that are noteworthy. First the use of a cognate noun with a verb, namely ἐφοβήθησαν φόβον, is sometimes described as a *Semitism*, meaning that this construction appears to reflect Hebrew rather than Greek idiom. Second, the ὅτι clause is epexegetical, further explaining the reason for the disciples' terror—only God has the power to command the wind and the waves; therefore who must Jesus be?
- Did you recognize the genitive absolute in sentence 9? In addition to the participle and the pronoun being in the genitive case, notice that the participle is plural, whereas the finite verb is singular. This clearly indicates that the subject of the participle and the finite verb cannot be the same. Notice also that the genitive absolute is best rendered as a dependent clause with a finite verb in English.

chapter **TWENTY-THREE**

THE INFINITIVE: *Forms and Functions*

You should complete these assignments after you have studied the material for chapter 23 in the textbook and memorized the required vocabulary, paradigms, and principal parts. Once you have completed these assignments to the best of your ability, check your work with the answer key.

For each of the following Greek forms, write out the specified components. Be sure to list all possibilities when applicable. Remember to indicate if a component does not apply for the inflected form by writing any of the following: N/A, n/a, or --.

inflected form	tense	voice	mood	pers	case	num	gender	lexical form	inflected meaning
φαγεῖν									
ποιῆσαι									
ἀπαγγεῖλαι									
ἔχειν									
ἄρξασθαι									
κρῖναι									
σωθῆναι									
γίνεσθαι									
κηρύξαι									
ἀποθανεῖν									

TRANSLATION

- For each of the following sentences, double underline each finite verb.
- Put brackets around every [prepositional phrase].
- Single underline each adjective.
- Above each adjective write its function: attributive (ATTR), substantival (SUB), or predicate (PRED).
- Highlight each subordinating conjunction and relative pronoun.
- Put a parenthesis around each (subordinate clause) or (relative clause).
- If applicable, draw an arrow from each relative pronoun to its antecedent.
- Put a square box around every nonfinite verb.
- Above each participle write its function: adverbial (ADV), attributive (ATTR), or substantival (SUB).
- If applicable, draw an arrow from the participle to the word it modifies.
- Translate the following sentences.

Pop-Up Lexicon

ἀπιστία, -ας, ἡ	unfaithfulness, unbelief
θανατόω	I kill, I put to death
Ῥώμη, -ης, ἡ	Rome
τελέω	I finish, I complete

1. οὐ δύναμαι ἐγὼ ποιεῖν ἀπ᾽ ἐμαυτοῦ οὐδέν· καθὼς ἀκούω κρίνω, καὶ ἡ κρίσις ἡ ἐμὴ δικαία ἐστίν, ὅτι οὐ ζητῶ τὸ θέλημα τὸ ἐμὸν ἀλλὰ τὸ θέλημα τοῦ πέμψαντός με.

2. καὶ βλέπομεν ὅτι οὐκ ἠδυνήθησαν εἰσελθεῖν δι᾽ ἀπιστίαν.

3. αὐτὸς δὲ Ἰησοῦς οὐκ ἐπίστευεν αὐτὸν αὐτοῖς διὰ τὸ αὐτὸν γινώσκειν πάντας καὶ ὅτι οὐ χρείαν εἶχεν ἵνα τις μαρτυρήσῃ περὶ τοῦ ἀνθρώπου.

4. οἱ δὲ ἀρχιερεῖς καὶ ὅλον τὸ συνέδριον ἐζήτουν κατὰ τοῦ Ἰησοῦ μαρτυρίαν εἰς τὸ θανατῶσαι αὐτόν, καὶ οὐχ ηὕρισκον.

5. λέγω γὰρ ὑμῖν ὅτι τοῦτο τὸ γεγραμμένον δεῖ τελεσθῆναι ἐν ἐμοί.

6. εἰ οὖν ἐγὼ ἔνιψα ὑμῶν τοὺς πόδας ὁ κύριος καὶ ὁ διδάσκαλος, καὶ ὑμεῖς ὀφείλετε ἀλλήλων νίπτειν τοὺς πόδας.

7. οὐκ ἔχετε διὰ τὸ μὴ αἰτεῖσθαι ὑμᾶς.

8. καὶ πάλιν ἤρξατο διδάσκειν παρὰ τὴν θάλασσαν.

9. μετὰ τὸ γενέσθαι με ἐκεῖ δεῖ με καὶ Ῥώμην ἰδεῖν.

10. καὶ ἐποίησεν δώδεκα . . . ἵνα ὦσιν μετ᾽ αὐτοῦ καὶ ἵνα ἀποστέλλῃ αὐτοὺς κηρύσσειν καὶ ἔχειν ἐξουσίαν ἐκβάλλειν τὰ δαιμόνια.

CORRECTION AND ASSESSMENT

Instructions

Once you have completed the parsing and translation exercises to the best of your ability, you may then look at the answer key. On this page, you will find spaces to assess any mistakes you made and to indicate the course of action you took to address the problem.

inflected form or sentence #	assessment	course of action

ANSWER KEY

Parsing

inflected form	tense	voice	mood	pers	case	num	gender	lexical form	inflected meaning
φαγεῖν	aor	act	inf	n/a	n/a	n/a	n/a	ἐσθίω	to eat
ποιῆσαι	aor	act	inf	n/a	n/a	n/a	n/a	ποιέω	to do
ἀπαγγεῖλαι	aor	act	inf	n/a	n/a	n/a	n/a	ἀπαγγέλλω	to send
ἔχειν	pres	act	inf	n/a	n/a	n/a	n/a	ἔχω	to have
ἄρξασθαι	aor	mid	inf	n/a	n/a	n/a	n/a	ἄρχω	to begin
κρῖναι	aor	act	inf	n/a	n/a	n/a	n/a	κρίνω	to judge
σωθῆναι	aor	pass	inf	n/a	n/a	n/a	n/a	σῴζω	to be saved
γίνεσθαι	pres	mid	inf	n/a	n/a	n/a	n/a	γίνομαι	to become
κηρύξαι	aor	act	inf	n/a	n/a	n/a	n/a	κηρύσσω	to preach
ἀποθανεῖν	aor	act	inf	n/a	n/a	n/a	n/a	ἀποθνήσκω	to die

Translation

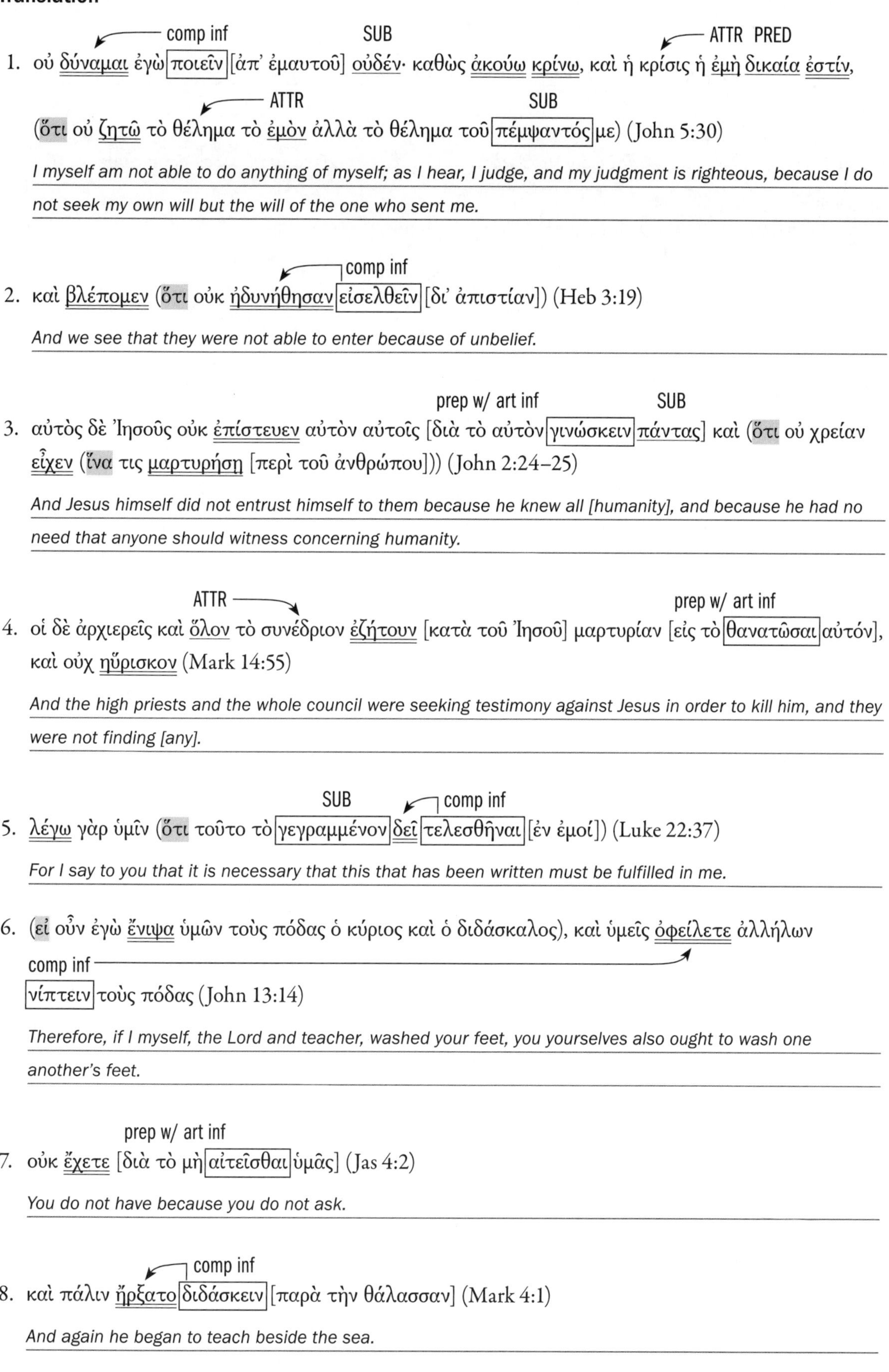

comp inf SUB ATTR PRED

1. οὐ δύναμαι ἐγὼ ποιεῖν [ἀπ' ἐμαυτοῦ] οὐδέν· καθὼς ἀκούω κρίνω, καὶ ἡ κρίσις ἡ ἐμὴ δικαία ἐστίν,

ATTR SUB

(ὅτι οὐ ζητῶ τὸ θέλημα τὸ ἐμὸν ἀλλὰ τὸ θέλημα τοῦ πέμψαντός με) (John 5:30)

I myself am not able to do anything of myself; as I hear, I judge, and my judgment is righteous, because I do not seek my own will but the will of the one who sent me.

comp inf

2. καὶ βλέπομεν (ὅτι οὐκ ἠδυνήθησαν εἰσελθεῖν [δι' ἀπιστίαν]) (Heb 3:19)

And we see that they were not able to enter because of unbelief.

prep w/ art inf SUB

3. αὐτὸς δὲ Ἰησοῦς οὐκ ἐπίστευεν αὐτὸν αὐτοῖς [διὰ τὸ αὐτὸν γινώσκειν πάντας] καὶ (ὅτι οὐ χρείαν εἶχεν (ἵνα τις μαρτυρήσῃ [περὶ τοῦ ἀνθρώπου])) (John 2:24–25)

And Jesus himself did not entrust himself to them because he knew all [humanity], and because he had no need that anyone should witness concerning humanity.

ATTR prep w/ art inf

4. οἱ δὲ ἀρχιερεῖς καὶ ὅλον τὸ συνέδριον ἐζήτουν [κατὰ τοῦ Ἰησοῦ] μαρτυρίαν [εἰς τὸ θανατῶσαι αὐτόν], καὶ οὐχ ηὕρισκον (Mark 14:55)

And the high priests and the whole council were seeking testimony against Jesus in order to kill him, and they were not finding [any].

SUB comp inf

5. λέγω γὰρ ὑμῖν (ὅτι τοῦτο τὸ γεγραμμένον δεῖ τελεσθῆναι [ἐν ἐμοί]) (Luke 22:37)

For I say to you that it is necessary that this that has been written must be fulfilled in me.

6. (εἰ οὖν ἐγὼ ἔνιψα ὑμῶν τοὺς πόδας ὁ κύριος καὶ ὁ διδάσκαλος), καὶ ὑμεῖς ὀφείλετε ἀλλήλων

comp inf

νίπτειν τοὺς πόδας (John 13:14)

Therefore, if I myself, the Lord and teacher, washed your feet, you yourselves also ought to wash one another's feet.

prep w/ art inf

7. οὐκ ἔχετε [διὰ τὸ μὴ αἰτεῖσθαι ὑμᾶς] (Jas 4:2)

You do not have because you do not ask.

comp inf

8. καὶ πάλιν ἤρξατο διδάσκειν [παρὰ τὴν θάλασσαν] (Mark 4:1)

And again he began to teach beside the sea.

prep w/ art inf — comp inf

9. [μετὰ τὸ γενέσθαι με ἐκεῖ] δεῖ με καὶ Ῥώμην ἰδεῖν (Acts 19:21)

After I have been there, it is necessary for me also to see Rome.

SUB — purpose — purpose — purpose

10. καὶ ἐποίησεν δώδεκα . . . (ἵνα ὦσιν [μετ᾽ αὐτοῦ]) καὶ (ἵνα ἀποστέλλῃ αὐτοὺς κηρύσσειν καὶ ἔχειν ἐξουσίαν ἐκβάλλειν τὰ δαιμόνια) (Mark 3:14–15)

And he appointed the Twelve . . . in order that they might be with him and in order that he might send them to preach and to have authority to throw out demons.

Additional Notes:

- In sentence 1, notice that the finite verb δύναμαι by itself begs the question "what?"—"I am [not] able to what?" This is a good clue that the infinitive is functioning as a *complementary infinitive*; namely, it completes the meaning of the finite verb. Notice also the verbal action or idea is communicated by the infinitive, not the finite verb, which functions almost like an auxillary. In other words, the focus here is on ποιεῖν, not on δύναμαι. This might be clearer with another verb, such as "to die"; in the clause δύναμαι ἀποθανεῖν, the focus is on the verbal action of dying (communicated by the infinitive ἀποθανεῖν), not the ability to do this action (communicated by the finite verb δύναμαι).
- Sentence 2 offers another example of a complementary infinitive. Notice again that the focus is on the wilderness generation's inability to *enter* [the promise of the land], which is communicated by the infinitive.
- In sentence 3, notice that the expression διὰ τὸ αὐτὸν γινώσκειν πάντας cannot be translated word for word—any attempt to do so yields an incomprehensible outcome. The expression διὰ τό + the infinitive must be memorized as indicating reason and is usually translated with "because" and a finite clause in English, such as "because he knows all [humanity]" in John 2:24 ("humanity" is implied from the overall context). Notice also that αὐτόν indicates the "subject" of the infinitive and in this case refers to Jesus. There is a range of options for the translation of ἄνθρωπος in this verse; in the overall context of John's Gospel, ἄνθρωπος indicates all human beings, so we have translated it "humanity." Some translations use an inclusively understood "man." It would also be possible to translate ἄνθρωπος as "people," although λάος is typically used to refer to the people of God in the GNT and the LXX, so we like to reserve "people" for λάος if possible. Finally, there is an implicit idea here that Jesus did not have need for anyone to testify to him about the nature of human beings, because he came to redeem fallen humanity and fully knew its fallen condition.
- Sentence 4 offers another good example of a preposition with an articular infinitive; the expression εἰς τό + infinitive must be memorized as indicating purpose. Because of the nature of English, "in order" can be followed by an infinitive, such as "in order to kill him." So this particular construction might not feel as idiomatic as other ones involving a preposition followed by an articular infinitive. Notice that αὐτόν here is functioning as the object of the infinitive.
- The use of δεῖ in sentence 5 is interesting. Δεῖ is called an *impersonal verb* because it does not have a specific grammatical subject and only occurs in the third-person singular. Notice the translation for

δεῖ—"it is necessary," where "it" does not have a specific subject referent. In the clause ὅτι τοῦτο τὸ γεγραμμένον δεῖ τελεσθῆναι ἐν ἐμοί, the phrase τοῦτο τὸ γεγραμμένον is functioning as the "subject" of the infinitive. This leads to the following translation: "that" (ὅτι) "it is necessary" (δεῖ) that (required by English) "this that has been written" (subject of the infinitive; τοῦτο τὸ γεγραμμένον) "be fulfilled" (infinitive; τελεσθῆναι) "in me" (ἐν ἐμοί). This translation is rather awkward in English, which likely explains why many English translations make τοῦτο τὸ γεγραμμένον the subject of the ὅτι *clause* (not the infinitive) and translate the entire clause something like the following: "That which is written must be fulfilled in me."

- Sentence 6 gives a good example of a first-class conditional. Recall that first-class conditionals assume a condition to be true for the sake of the argument. In this example, the condition (or protasis) is indeed true, which is why many English translations have "because" or "since" rather than "if." Recall also that the article can function in a similar manner to a personal pronoun indicating possession, so the subject of the first clause could also be translated "your Lord and teacher."
- Sentence 7 offers another example of διὰ τό + an infinitive. Notice also that the negation used with infinitives is μή, not οὐ. Finally, notice that ὑμᾶς functions as the "subject" of the infinitive.
- Sentence 9 provides an example of a different preposition plus articular-infinitive construction: μετὰ τό + infinitive. Here με functions as the "subject" of the infinitive. By now it should be clear that these expressions must be committed to memory.
- Sentence 10 gives several "textbook" examples of a purpose infinitive modifying a subjunctive, and even one purpose infinitive modifying a previous purpose infinitive (or more precisely, the infinitival clause ἔχειν ἐξουσίαν). (Alternatively, you could think of the infinitive ἐκβάλλειν "completing" the meaning of ἐξουσίαν—authority to cast out.) Personally, this is one my favorite verses. Notice the first reason that Jesus chose the Twelve was so that they could be with him. Secondarily, they are called to preach and to exercise authority over demons. Too often we get this reversed—we think that Jesus primarily calls people for specific ministries, and we might not even think about the fact that he calls us to be with him. Of course, it pleases him to use his followers in specific ways, but we are primarily called to be with him—everything else flows from that. Mark 3:14–15 makes these priorities clear.

chapter TWENTY-FOUR

μι VERBS: *Finite Forms*

You should complete these assignments after you have studied the material for chapter 24 in the textbook and memorized the required vocabulary, paradigms, and principal parts. Once you have completed these assignments to the best of your ability, check your work with the answer key.

For each of the following Greek forms, write out the specified components. Be sure to list all possibilities when applicable. Remember to indicate if a component does not apply for the inflected form by writing any of the following: N/A, n/a, or --.

inflected form	tense	voice	mood	pers	case	num	gender	lexical form	inflected meaning
δός									
ἀπέδωκεν									
ἀπολλύμεθα									
συνιᾶσιν									
ἀφίησιν									
θῶ									
παραδιδῷ									
συνέστηκεν									
ἑστήκατε									
ἐπίθες									

TRANSLATION

- For each of the following sentences, double underline each finite verb.
- Put brackets around every [prepositional phrase].
- Single underline each adjective.
- Above each adjective write its function: attributive (ATTR), substantival (SUB), or predicate (PRED).
- Highlight each subordinating conjunction and relative pronoun.
- Put a parenthesis around each (subordinate clause) or (relative clause).
- If applicable, draw an arrow from each relative pronoun to its antecedent.
- Put a square box around every nonfinite verb.
- Above each participle write its function: adverbial (ADV), attributive (ATTR), or substantival (SUB).
- If applicable, draw an arrow from the participle to the word it modifies.
- Translate the following sentences.

Pop-Up Lexicon

ἀδικία, -ας, ἡ	unrighteousness, injustice, evil
ἀνατίθημι	I lay before, I present, I communicate
διαλλάσσομαι	I am reconciled
εἰσφέρω	I bring in, I lead in
κἀκεῖ	and there
κλείς, κλειδός, ἡ	key
ὅπλον, -ου, τό	instrument, weapon

1. βλέπετε οὖν πῶς ἀκούετε ὃς ἂν γὰρ ἔχῃ, δοθήσεται αὐτῷ· καὶ ὃς ἂν μὴ ἔχῃ, καὶ ὃ δοκεῖ ἔχειν ἀρθήσεται ἀπ᾽ αὐτοῦ.

2. δότε κἀμοὶ τὴν ἐξουσίαν ταύτην ἵνα ᾧ ἐὰν ἐπιθῶ τὰς χεῖρας λαμβάνῃ πνεῦμα ἅγιον.

3. μηδὲ παριστάνετε τὰ μέλη ὑμῶν ὅπλα ἀδικίας τῇ ἁμαρτίᾳ, ἀλλὰ παραστήσατε ἑαυτοὺς τῷ θεῷ ὡσεὶ ἐκ νεκρῶν ζῶντας καὶ τὰ μέλη ὑμῶν ὅπλα δικαιοσύνης τῷ θεῷ.

4. καὶ ἀνεθέμην αὐτοῖς τὸ εὐαγγέλιον ὃ κηρύσσω ἐν τοῖς ἔθνεσιν.

5. καὶ ἄφες ἡμῖν τὰς ἁμαρτίας ἡμῶν, καὶ γὰρ αὐτοὶ ἀφίομεν παντὶ ὀφείλοντι ἡμῖν· καὶ μὴ εἰσενέγκῃς ἡμᾶς εἰς πειρασμόν.

6. ἀπεκρίθη αὐτοῖς ὁ Ἰωάννης λέγων, ἐγὼ βαπτίζω ἐν ὕδατι· μέσος ὑμῶν ἕστηκεν ὃν ὑμεῖς οὐκ οἴδατε.

7. διὰ τοῦτό με ὁ πατὴρ ἀγαπᾷ ὅτι ἐγὼ τίθημι τὴν ψυχήν μου, ἵνα πάλιν λάβω αὐτήν.

8. . . . ἵνα βλέποντες βλέπωσιν καὶ μὴ ἴδωσιν, καὶ ἀκούοντες ἀκούωσιν καὶ μὴ συνιῶσιν, μήποτε ἐπιστρέψωσιν καὶ ἀφεθῇ αὐτοῖς.

9. δώσω σοι τὰς κλεῖδας τῆς βασιλείας τῶν οὐρανῶν, καὶ ὃ ἐὰν δήσῃς ἐπὶ τῆς γῆς ἔσται δεδεμένον ἐν τοῖς οὐρανοῖς, καὶ ὃ ἐὰν λύσῃς ἐπὶ τῆς γῆς ἔσται λελυμένον ἐν τοῖς οὐρανοῖς.

10. ἐὰν οὖν προσφέρῃς τὸ δῶρόν σου ἐπὶ τὸ θυσιαστήριον κἀκεῖ μνησθῇς ὅτι ὁ ἀδελφός σου ἔχει τι κατὰ σοῦ, ἄφες ἐκεῖ τὸ δῶρόν σου ἔμπροσθεν τοῦ θυσιαστηρίου καὶ ὕπαγε πρῶτον διαλλάγηθι τῷ ἀδελφῷ σου.

CORRECTION AND ASSESSMENT

Instructions

Once you have completed the parsing and translation exercises to the best of your ability, you may then look at the answer key. On this page, you will find spaces to assess any mistakes you made and to indicate the course of action you took to address the problem.

inflected form or sentence #	assessment	course of action

inflected form or sentence #	assessment	course of action

ANSWER KEY

Parsing

inflected form	tense	voice	mood	pers	case	num	gender	lexical form	inflected meaning
δός	aor	act	impv	2nd	n/a	sg	n/a	δίδωμι	(you sg) give!
ἀπέδωκεν	aor	act	ind	3rd	n/a	sg	n/a	ἀποδίδωμι	he/she/it gave away
ἀπολλύμεθα	pres	mid pass	ind	1st	n/a	pl	n/a	ἀπόλλυμι	we perish for ourselves we die
συνιᾶσιν	pres	act	ind	3rd	n/a	pl	n/a	συνίημι	they understand
ἀφίησιν	pres	act	ind	3rd	n/a	sg	n/a	ἀφίημι	he/she/it lets go
θῶ	aor	act	subj	1st	n/a	sg	n/a	τίθημι	I would put
παραδιδῷ	pres	act	subj	3rd	n/a	sg	n/a	παραδίδωμι	he/she/it might hand over
συνέστηκεν	pf	act	ind	3rd	n/a	sg	n/a	συνίστημι	he/she/it has demonstrated
ἑστήκατε	pf	act	ind	2nd	n/a	pl	n/a	ἵστημι	you (pl) stand
ἐπίθες	aor	act	impv	2nd	n/a	sg	n/a	ἐπιτίθημι	(you sg) put upon!

Translation

1. βλέπετε οὖν πῶς ἀκούετε· (ὃς ἂν γὰρ ἔχῃ), δοθήσεται αὐτῷ· καὶ (ὃς ἂν μὴ ἔχῃ), καὶ (ὃ δοκεῖ
comp inf
ἔχειν) ἀρθήσεται [ἀπ' αὐτοῦ] (Luke 8:18)

   Therefore, see how you hear: For whoever has, it will be given to him; and whoever does not have, even what he supposes to have will be taken away from him.

ATTR

2. δότε κἀμοὶ τὴν ἐξουσίαν ταύτην (ἵνα (ᾧ ἐὰν ἐπιθῶ τὰς χεῖρας) λαμβάνῃ πνεῦμα ἅγιον) (Acts 8:19)

   Give also to me this authority, in order that on whomever I lay my hands may receive the Holy Spirit.

3. μηδὲ παριστάνετε τὰ μέλη ὑμῶν ὅπλα ἀδικίας τῇ ἁμαρτίᾳ, ἀλλὰ παραστήσατε ἑαυτοὺς

SUB SUB

τῷ θεῷ ὡσεὶ [ἐκ νεκρῶν] ζῶντας καὶ τὰ μέλη ὑμῶν ὅπλα δικαιοσύνης τῷ θεῷ (Rom 6:13)

But do not present your members as instruments of unrighteousness to sin, but present yourselves to God as those who are alive from the dead and your members as instruments of righteousness to God.

4. καὶ ἀνεθέμην αὐτοῖς τὸ εὐαγγέλιον (ὃ κηρύσσω [ἐν τοῖς ἔθνεσιν]) (Gal 2:2)

And I communicated to them the gospel, which I preached among the gentiles.

ATTR → SUB

5. καὶ ἄφες ἡμῖν τὰς ἁμαρτίας ἡμῶν, καὶ γὰρ αὐτοὶ ἀφίομεν παντὶ ὀφείλοντι ἡμῖν· καὶ μὴ εἰσενέγκῃς ἡμᾶς [εἰς πειρασμόν] (Luke 11:4)

And forgive us our sins, for we ourselves also forgive all who owe us; and do not lead us to temptation.

ADV

6. ἀπεκρίθη αὐτοῖς ὁ Ἰωάννης λέγων, ἐγὼ βαπτίζω [ἐν ὕδατι]· [μέσος ὑμῶν] ἕστηκεν (ὃν ὑμεῖς οὐκ οἴδατε) (John 1:26)

John answered them, saying, "I myself am baptizing with water; there stands [someone] in your midst whom you do not know."

7. [διὰ τοῦτό] με ὁ πατὴρ ἀγαπᾷ (ὅτι ἐγὼ τίθημι τὴν ψυχήν μου, (ἵνα πάλιν λάβω αὐτήν)) (John 10:17)

Therefore, the Father loves me, because I myself lay down my life, in order that I may take it up again.

ADV → ADV →

8. . . . (ἵνα βλέποντες βλέπωσιν καὶ μὴ ἴδωσιν, καὶ ἀκούοντες ἀκούωσιν καὶ μὴ συνιῶσιν), μήποτε ἐπιστρέψωσιν καὶ ἀφεθῇ αὐτοῖς (Mark 4:12)

. . . in order that seeing they might see and not perceive, and hearing they might hear and not understand, unless they might turn and it might be forgiven to them.

9. δώσω σοι τὰς κλεῖδας τῆς βασιλείας τῶν οὐρανῶν, καὶ (ὃ ἐὰν δήσῃς [ἐπὶ τῆς γῆς]) ἔσται

ADV; periphrastic ADV; periphrastic

δεδεμένον [ἐν τοῖς οὐρανοῖς], καὶ (ὃ ἐὰν λύσῃς [ἐπὶ τῆς γῆς]) ἔσται λελυμένον [ἐν τοῖς οὐρανοῖς] (Matt 16:19)

I will give to you the keys of the kingdom of heaven, and whatever you bind on earth will be bound in heaven, and whatever you release on earth will be released in heaven.

10. (ἐὰν οὖν προσφέρῃς τὸ δῶρόν σου [ἐπὶ τὸ θυσιαστήριον] κἀκεῖ μνησθῇς (ὅτι ὁ ἀδελφός σου ἔχει τι [κατὰ σοῦ])), ἄφες ἐκεῖ τὸ δῶρόν σου [ἔμπροσθεν τοῦ θυσιαστηρίου] καὶ ὕπαγε πρῶτον διαλλάγηθι τῷ ἀδελφῷ σου (Matt 5:23–24)

Therefore, if you bring your gift to the altar and there you remember that your brother has something against you, leave your gift there before the altar and depart; first be reconciled with your brother.

Additional Notes:

- In sentence 1, βλέπετε could also be rendered "pay attention to."
- In sentence 1, the relative clause ὃς ἂν γὰρ ἔχῃ is functioning as the "subject" of Jesus's comments, but notice that this clause is not the grammatical subject of δοθήσεται; in other words, Jesus is not saying, "whoever has will be given to him . . . ," which is nonsensical. Instead Jesus is referring to a person (ostensibly from among the audience) with ὃς ἂν γὰρ ἔχῃ, and the "it" implied here refers to the "mystery of the kingdom," which is inferred from the overall context. This use of the nominative (ὃς ἂν γὰρ ἔχῃ) is sometimes called a *hanging nominative*, where a construction in the nominative is the understood subject, but another entity is the actual grammatical subject. Notice also that the antecedent for the relative pronoun ὅ is not stated explicitly but must be inferred from the overall context. Here this probably implies some type of authority or knowledge that a person might suppose to possess (apart from the true kingdom) that will be taken away.
- The relative clause ᾧ ἐὰν ἐπιθῶ τὰς χεῖρας in sentence 2 is a good example of a relative clause functioning substantivally, here as the subject of the ἵνα clause.
- Did you recognize that κἀμοί was an inflected form of κἀγώ in sentence 2? Also notice the possessive understanding of the article in this sentence: in this context, τὰς χεῖρας could only be translated as "my hands."
- You may have been a bit confused by the series of accusatives in sentence 3. These are sometimes called *double accusatives*, but they are more properly understood as an *object complement*. The verb παρίστημι implies that one entity will be presented as something else—in this case τὰ μέλη ὑμῶν being presented as ὅπλα ἀδικίας. Object complements frequently occur with verbs that indicate designating, appointing, naming, calling, presenting, etc. Notice that the clause παριστάνετε τὰ μέλη ὑμῶν does not fully make sense by itself and seems to be lacking something. This is why the second accusative, ὅπλα ἀδικίας, is called an object complement; it "completes" the meaning of the object of the verb, τὰ μέλη ὑμῶν, the first object.
- Notice that the participle ζῶντας in sentence 3 is accusative plural masculine. There is no substantive around that matches this participle in case, number, and gender, so it must be functioning substantivally. But notice also that ἑαυτούς is also accusative plural masculine. Together with ὡσεὶ, the fact that both the reflexive pronoun and the participle are in the same case, number, and gender indicates that the recipients of Paul's letter are being compared to something; in this case, they (who are alive) are being compared to those who are actually dead. This participle could be translated "living," but "living from the dead" doesn't really make sense; hence the translation "alive from the dead."
- In sentence 4, English style leads to the rendering of κηρύσσω as a simple past, "I preached." The present-tense verb κηρύσσω communicates imperfective aspect, which may indicate here that Paul's work of preaching the gospel among the gentiles is ongoing from the point of view when he wrote his letter to the Galatians.
- In the opening part of sentence 5 (καὶ ἄφες ἡμῖν τὰς ἁμαρτίας ἡμῶν), it is helpful to pay attention to the cases: τὰς ἁμαρτίας is in the accusative and is clearly functioning as the direct object of the finite verb ἄφες, and ἡμῖν is in the dative case and is clearly functioning as the indirect object. The idea is one of a debt (τὰς ἁμαρτίας) that is being canceled on behalf of someone (ἡμῖν). Notice also that καί is between two unequal syntactic units; hence the translation "also" here. Next, although παντί could be masculine or neuter, the context here indicates that it is masculine, referring to people. This verb,

ἀφίημι, frequently takes an inanimate object in the accusative case and a personal object in the dative case, as we see in this verse. Finally, notice the second-person aorist subjunctive that is functioning volitionally parallel to an imperative.

- The use of λαμβάνω in sentence 7 is a bit idiomatic. The context makes it clear that this verb means something like "take up" here.
- In sentence 8, the implied object of ἀφεθῇ must be inferred from the context. In this citation from Isaiah 6:9–10, the object is best understood as sin, which is reflected in several English versions. English requires some type of object, which is reflected in the supplied "it" in our translation. Other English versions avoid this awkwardness by rendering the personal pronoun αὐτοῖς as the subject of the clause: "Lest they be forgiven."
- We have noted the use of οὐρανός in previous chapters. New Testament writers in general, and Matthew in particular (see sentence 9), use the plural form based on the corresponding Hebrew expression, which is plural.
- Sentence 9 contains a good example of a relative clause (ὃ ἐὰν δήσῃς) functioning as the subject of a clause. It also contains a good example of a periphrastic construction: ἔσται δεδεμένον. These same constructions are found in the parallel clause with λύω.

chapter TWENTY-FIVE

μι VERBS: *Nonfinite Forms*

You should complete these assignments after you have studied the material for chapter 25 in the textbook and memorized the required vocabulary, paradigms, and principal parts. Once you have completed these assignments to the best of your ability, check your work with the answer key.

For each of the following Greek forms, write out the specified components. Be sure to list all possibilities when applicable. Remember to indicate if a component does not apply for the inflected form by writing any of the following: N/A, n/a, or --.

inflected form	tense	voice	mood	pers	case	num	gender	lexical form	inflected meaning
ἀφέντες									
διδόμενον									
ἀπολέσαι									
ἑστῶτες									
θεῖναι									
συνιέντος									
δοθῆναι									
ἀναστᾶσα									
στῆναι									
θείς									

TRANSLATION

- For each of the following sentences, double underline each finite verb.
- Put brackets around every [prepositional phrase].
- Single underline each adjective.
- Above each adjective write its function: attributive (ATTR), substantival (SUB), or predicate (PRED).
- Highlight each subordinating conjunction and relative pronoun.
- Put a parenthesis around each (subordinate clause) or (relative clause).
- If applicable, draw an arrow from each relative pronoun to its antecedent.
- Put a square box around every nonfinite verb.
- Above each participle write its function: adverbial (ADV), attributive (ATTR), or substantival (SUB).
- If applicable, draw an arrow from the participle to the word it modifies.
- Translate the following sentences.

Pop-Up Lexicon

δύνω	I set (of the sun)
λόγιον, -ου, τό	word, message, oracle
μωρία, -ας, ἡ	foolishness
Σινᾶ	Sinai
συστρέφω	I gather, I come together

1. . . . ἵνα δὲ εἰδῆτε ὅτι ἐξουσίαν ἔχει ὁ υἱὸς τοῦ ἀνθρώπου ἐπὶ τῆς γῆς ἀφιέναι ἁμαρτίας.

2. οὗτός ἐστιν ὁ γενόμενος ἐν τῇ ἐκκλησίᾳ ἐν τῇ ἐρήμῳ μετὰ τοῦ ἀγγέλου τοῦ λαλοῦντος αὐτῷ ἐν τῷ ὄρει Σινᾶ καὶ τῶν πατέρων ἡμῶν, ὃς ἐδέξατο λόγια ζῶντα δοῦναι ἡμῖν.

3. καὶ προσκαλεσάμενος αὐτοὺς ἐν παραβολαῖς ἔλεγεν αὐτοῖς πῶς δύναται σατανᾶς σατανᾶν ἐκβάλλειν; καὶ ἐὰν βασιλεία ἐφ' ἑαυτὴν μερισθῇ, οὐ δύναται σταθῆναι ἡ βασιλεία ἐκείνη.

4. ἦλθεν γὰρ ὁ υἱὸς τοῦ ἀνθρώπου ζητῆσαι καὶ σῶσαι τὸ ἀπολωλός.

5. πρὸ δὲ τούτων πάντων ἐπιβαλοῦσιν ἐφ' ὑμᾶς τὰς χεῖρας αὐτῶν καὶ διώξουσιν, παραδιδόντες εἰς τὰς συναγωγὰς καὶ φυλακάς.

6. ὁ λόγος γὰρ ὁ τοῦ σταυροῦ τοῖς μὲν ἀπολλυμένοις μωρία ἐστίν, τοῖς δὲ σῳζομένοις ἡμῖν δύναμις θεοῦ ἐστιν.

7. συστρεφομένων δὲ αὐτῶν ἐν τῇ Γαλιλαίᾳ εἶπεν αὐτοῖς ὁ Ἰησοῦς, μέλλει ὁ υἱὸς τοῦ ἀνθρώπου παραδίδοσθαι εἰς χεῖρας ἀνθρώπων, καὶ ἀποκτενοῦσιν αὐτόν, καὶ τῇ τρίτῃ ἡμέρᾳ ἐγερθήσεται.

8. δύνοντος δὲ τοῦ ἡλίου ἅπαντες ὅσοι εἶχον ἀσθενοῦντας . . . ἤγαγον αὐτοὺς πρὸς αὐτόν· ὁ δὲ ἑνὶ ἑκάστῳ αὐτῶν τὰς χεῖρας ἐπιτιθεὶς ἐθεράπευεν αὐτούς.

9. ὅρα γάρ φησιν, ποιήσεις πάντα κατὰ τὸν τύπον τὸν δειχθέντα σοι ἐν τῷ ὄρει.

CORRECTION AND ASSESSMENT

Instructions

Once you have completed the parsing and translation exercises to the best of your ability, you may then look at the answer key. On this page, you will find spaces to assess any mistakes you made and to indicate the course of action you took to address the problem.

inflected form or sentence #	assessment	course of action

ANSWER KEY

Parsing

inflected form	tense	voice	mood	pers	case	num	gender	lexical form	inflected meaning
ἀφέντες	aor	act	ptc	n/a	nom	pl	masc	ἀφίημι	those who let go
διδόμενον	pres	mid mid mid pass pass pass	ptc	n/a	acc nom acc acc nom acc	sg	masc neut neut masc neut neut	δίδωμι	one who gives for himself that which gives that which gives one who is given that which is given that which is given
ἀπολέσαι	aor	act	inf	n/a	n/a	n/a	n/a	ἀπόλλυμι	to destroy
ἑστῶτες	pf	act	ptc	n/a	nom	pl	masc	ἵστημι	those who stand
θεῖναι	aor	act	inf	n/a	n/a	n/a	n/a	τίθημι	to place
συνιέντος	pres	act	ptc	n/a	gen	sg	masc neut	συνίημι	of one who understands of that which understands
δοθῆναι	aor	pass	inf	n/a	n/a	n/a	n/a	δίδωμι	to be given
ἀναστᾶσα	pres	act	ptc	n/a	nom	sg	fem	ἀνίστημι	one (fem) who raises
στῆναι	aor	act	inf	n/a	n/a	n/a	n/a	ἵστημι	to stand
θείς	aor	act	ptc	n/a	nom	sg	masc	τίθημι	one who places

Translation

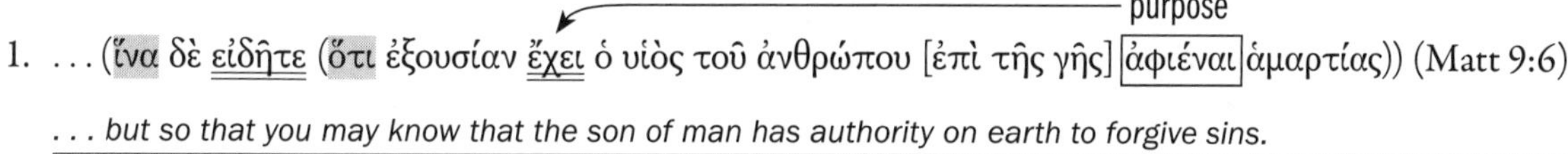

. . . but so that you may know that the son of man has authority on earth to forgive sins.

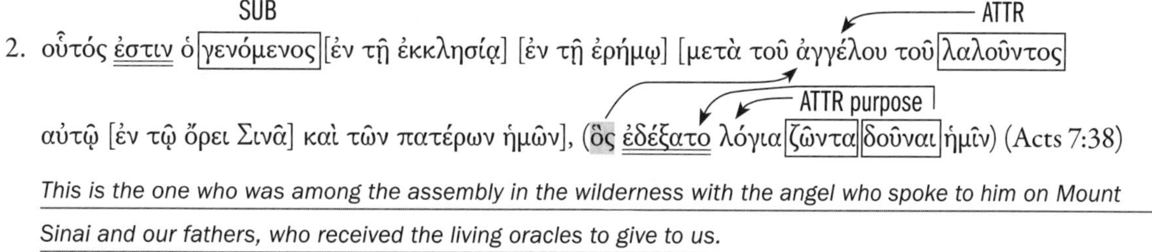

This is the one who was among the assembly in the wilderness with the angel who spoke to him on Mount Sinai and our fathers, who received the living oracles to give to us.

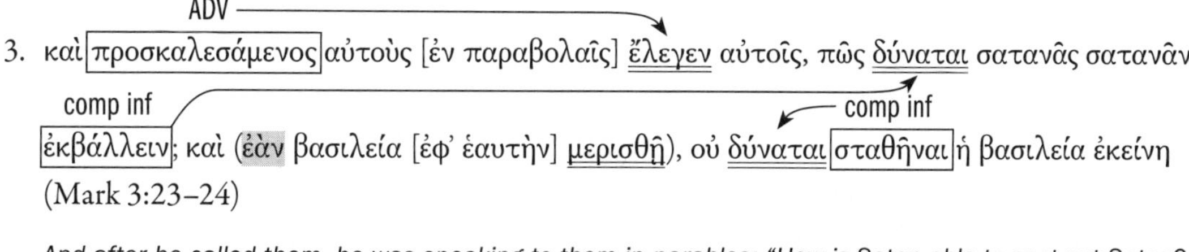

And after he called them, he was speaking to them in parables: "How is Satan able to cast out Satan? And if a kingdom is divided against itself, that kingdom is not able to stand."

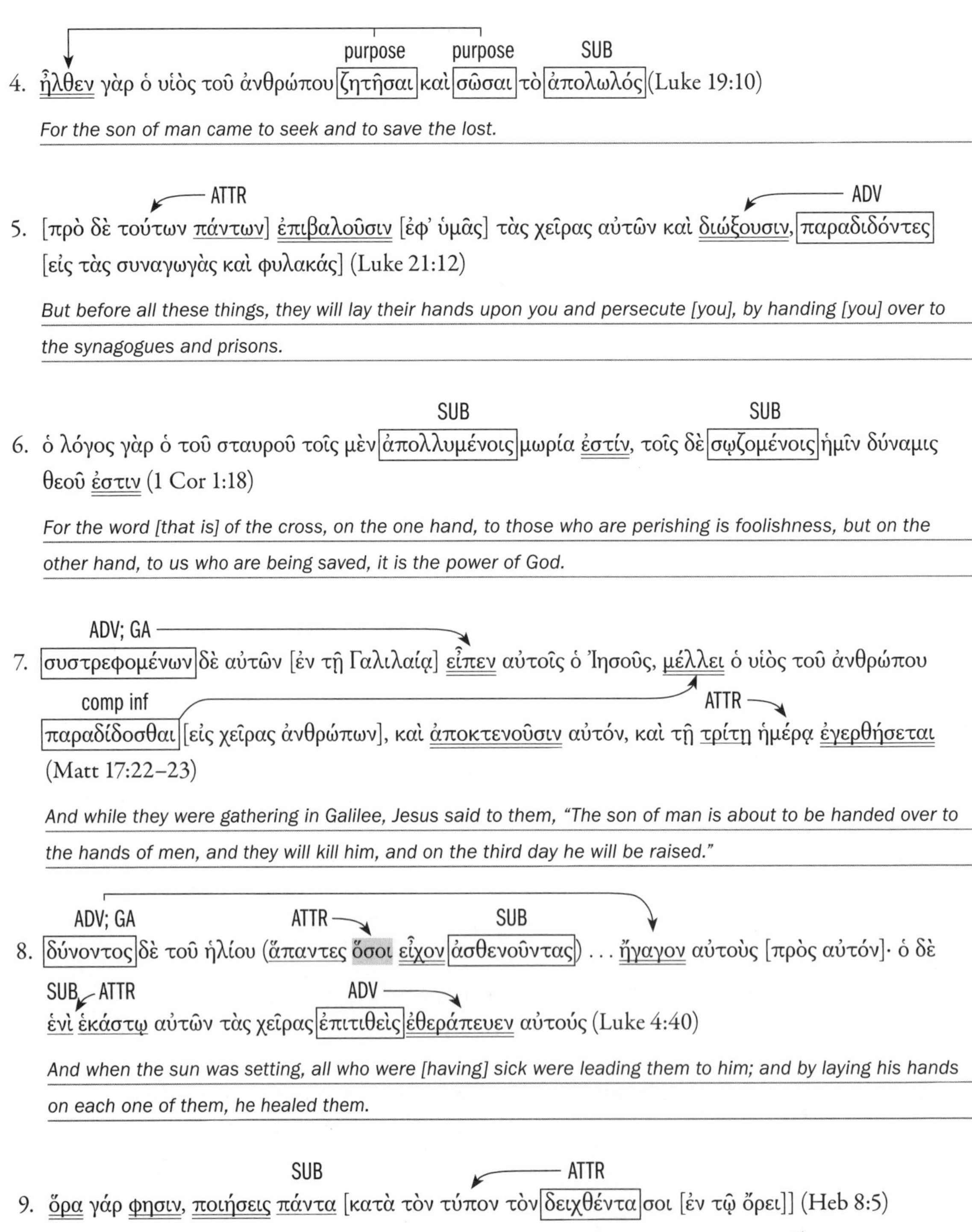

purpose purpose SUB
4. ἦλθεν γὰρ ὁ υἱὸς τοῦ ἀνθρώπου ζητῆσαι καὶ σῶσαι τὸ ἀπολωλός (Luke 19:10)
For the son of man came to seek and to save the lost.
ATTR ADV
5. [πρὸ δὲ τούτων πάντων] ἐπιβαλοῦσιν [ἐφ' ὑμᾶς] τὰς χεῖρας αὐτῶν καὶ διώξουσιν, παραδιδόντες [εἰς τὰς συναγωγὰς καὶ φυλακάς] (Luke 21:12)
But before all these things, they will lay their hands upon you and persecute [you], by handing [you] over to the synagogues and prisons.
SUB SUB
6. ὁ λόγος γὰρ ὁ τοῦ σταυροῦ τοῖς μὲν ἀπολλυμένοις μωρία ἐστίν, τοῖς δὲ σῳζομένοις ἡμῖν δύναμις θεοῦ ἐστιν (1 Cor 1:18)
For the word [that is] of the cross, on the one hand, to those who are perishing is foolishness, but on the other hand, to us who are being saved, it is the power of God.
ADV; GA
comp inf
ATTR
7. συστρεφομένων δὲ αὐτῶν [ἐν τῇ Γαλιλαίᾳ] εἶπεν αὐτοῖς ὁ Ἰησοῦς, μέλλει ὁ υἱὸς τοῦ ἀνθρώπου παραδίδοσθαι [εἰς χεῖρας ἀνθρώπων], καὶ ἀποκτενοῦσιν αὐτόν, καὶ τῇ τρίτῃ ἡμέρᾳ ἐγερθήσεται (Matt 17:22–23)
And while they were gathering in Galilee, Jesus said to them, "The son of man is about to be handed over to the hands of men, and they will kill him, and on the third day he will be raised."
ADV; GA ATTR SUB
SUB ATTR ADV
8. δύνοντος δὲ τοῦ ἡλίου (ἅπαντες ὅσοι εἶχον ἀσθενοῦντας) . . . ἤγαγον αὐτοὺς [πρὸς αὐτόν]· ὁ δὲ ἑνὶ ἑκάστῳ αὐτῶν τὰς χεῖρας ἐπιτιθεὶς ἐθεράπευεν αὐτούς (Luke 4:40)
And when the sun was setting, all who were [having] sick were leading them to him; and by laying his hands on each one of them, he healed them.
SUB ATTR
9. ὅρα γάρ φησιν, ποιήσεις πάντα [κατὰ τὸν τύπον τὸν δειχθέντα σοι [ἐν τῷ ὄρει]] (Heb 8:5)
"For see [that]," he said, "you will make all things according to the pattern which has been shown to you on the mountain."

Additional Notes:

- Sentence 1 offers a good example of a ὅτι clause indicating the content of the finite verb εἰδῆτε.
- Although sentence 2 (Acts 7:38) can look a bit intimidating, if you focus on identifying basic syntactic units and identifying the antecedent for the relative pronoun, the syntax of this verse is straightforward—even if there is a lot going on!

- Sentence 3 contains two good examples of complementary infinitives. The verb δύναμαι is frequently, though not always, followed by a complementary infinitive.
- Sentence 4 offers "textbook" examples of the function of an anarthrous infinitive to indicate purpose.
- In sentence 5, both διώξουσιν and παραδιδόντες can be used intransitively in Greek, whereas English requires some object for these verbs. The overall context makes it clear that those who are being addressed are the "object" of these verbs, which is reflected in the addition of "[you]."
- Sentence 6 is a good example of parallelism. If we line up the corresponding syntactic units, this becomes clear:

ὁ λόγος γὰρ ὁ τοῦ σταυροῦ	τοῖς	μὲν	ἀπολλυμένοις	μωρία ἐστίν,
	τοῖς	δὲ	σῳζομένοις ἡμῖν	δύναμις θεοῦ ἐστιν.

- In our translation of sentence 6, you can see that "it" in the second part of the translation must clearly refer to "the word [that is] of the cross." You will also notice that many English versions simply translate the initial noun phrase as "the word of the cross," which is a more natural reading in English. This is perfectly acceptable. We have added "[that is]" to make it clear that this is a second attributive position construction, not a genitival modifier and a head noun.
- Did you catch the genitive absolute at the beginning of sentence 7? Notice also that the substantive χεῖρας is definite even though it is anarthrous. Frequently the object of a preposition does not have an article. It is clear from the context, however, that this substantive is definite, which is reflected in the translation.
- Just to keep you on your toes, there is another genitive absolute in sentence 8. The construction ἅπαντες ὅσοι is interesting; ὅσοι is a correlative pronoun, which can be translated here "as many as," but it is modified by the adjective ἅπαντες. A literalistic translation would be awkward ("all as many as"), but the overall sense is clear. In this context, ὅσοι is functioning like a relative pronoun, which is indicated in the translation.
- Also in sentence 8, the use of εἶχον and the participle ἀσθενοῦντας is a bit unusual. We might have expected a periphrastic construction here. The participle ἀσθενοῦντας could be translated "being weak," or "being sick." But trying to have this translation with the imperfect εἶχον is a bit awkward, so the participle has been translated like a noun.
- The beginning of sentence 9 might seem a bit confusing, but the key is to recognize the switch in person. The verse opens with the second person (ὅρα), switches to the third person (φησιν), and then switches back to the second person (ποιήσεις). The second person is part of direct discourse, and the third person indicates who is speaking. To make this clearer, we have added quotation marks per English convention. Although you have learned that one of the glosses for ὁράω is "I see," the meanings "pay attention to" or "be aware that" are also possible. This is reflected in the addition of "[that]" after the imperative ὅρα.

chapter TWENTY-SIX

THE OPTATIVE: *Forms and Functions*

You should complete these assignments after you have studied the material for chapter 26 in the textbook and memorized the required vocabulary, paradigms, and principal parts. Once you have completed these assignments to the best of your ability, check your work with the answer key.

For each of the following Greek forms, write out the specified components. Be sure to list all possibilities when applicable. Remember to indicate if a component does not apply for the inflected form by writing any of the following: N/A, n/a, or --. Since this is the last chapter that presents new forms, the following words also give you a chance to review previously assigned forms.

inflected form	tense	voice	mood	pers	case	num	gender	lexical form	inflected meaning
πληρώσαι									
ἀγαπᾶτε									
φάγοι									
ἠδυνήθημεν									
ποιήσω									
εὕροιεν									
ἐπερίσσευον									
ἔχοι									
πρόσευξαι									
παθοῦσα									

TRANSLATION

- For each of the following sentences, double underline each finite verb.
- Put brackets around every [prepositional phrase].
- Single underline each adjective.
- Above each adjective write its function: attributive (ATTR), substantival (SUB), or predicate (PRED).
- Highlight each subordinating conjunction and relative pronoun.
- Put a parenthesis around each (subordinate clause) or (relative clause).
- If applicable, draw an arrow from each relative pronoun to its antecedent.
- Put a square box around every nonfinite verb.
- Above each participle write its function: adverbial (ADV), attributive (ATTR), or substantival (SUB).
- If applicable, draw an arrow from the participle to the word it modifies.
- Translate the following sentences.

Pop-Up Lexicon

ἀμέμπτως	blamelessly
δούλη, -ης, ἡ	female slave, female servant
Μαριάμ, ἡ	Mary

1. ἐπιτιμήσαι σοι κύριος.

2. δῴη αὐτῷ ὁ κύριος εὑρεῖν ἔλεος παρὰ κυρίου ἐν ἐκείνῃ τῇ ἡμέρᾳ.

3. αὐτὸς δὲ ὁ κύριος ἡμῶν Ἰησοῦς Χριστὸς καὶ ὁ θεὸς ὁ πατὴρ ἡμῶν ὁ ἀγαπήσας ἡμᾶς καὶ δοὺς . . .

   ἐλπίδα ἀγαθὴν ἐν χάριτι, παρακαλέσαι ὑμῶν τὰς καρδίας.

4. τί οὖν; ἁμαρτήσωμεν, ὅτι οὐκ ἐσμὲν ὑπὸ νόμον ἀλλὰ ὑπὸ χάριν; μὴ γένοιτο.

5. ὁ δὲ θεὸς τῆς ἐλπίδος πληρώσαι ὑμᾶς πάσης χαρᾶς καὶ εἰρήνης ἐν τῷ πιστεύειν, εἰς τὸ περισσεύειν ὑμᾶς ἐν τῇ ἐλπίδι ἐν δυνάμει πνεύματος ἁγίου.

____

____

6. εἶπεν δὲ Μαριάμ, ἰδοὺ ἡ δούλη κυρίου· γένοιτό μοι κατὰ τὸ ῥῆμά σου. καὶ ἀπῆλθεν ἀπ᾽ αὐτῆς ὁ ἄγγελος.

____

____

7. αὐτὸς δὲ ὁ θεὸς τῆς εἰρήνης ἁγιάσαι ὑμᾶς . . . ὑμῶν τὸ πνεῦμα καὶ ἡ ψυχὴ καὶ τὸ σῶμα ἀμέμπτως ἐν τῇ παρουσίᾳ τοῦ κυρίου ἡμῶν Ἰησοῦ χριστοῦ τηρηθείη.

____

____

8. ἀλλ᾽ εἰ καὶ πάσχοιτε διὰ δικαιοσύνην, μακάριοι.

____

CORRECTION AND ASSESSMENT

Instructions

Once you have completed the parsing and translation exercises to the best of your ability, you may then look at the answer key. On this page, you will find spaces to assess any mistakes you made and to indicate the course of action you took to address the problem.

inflected form or sentence #	assessment	course of action

inflected form or sentence #	assessment	course of action

ANSWER KEY

Parsing

inflected form	tense	voice	mood	pers	case	num	gender	lexical form	inflected meaning
πληρώσαι	aor	act	opt	3rd	n/a	sg	n/a	πληρόω	may he/she/it fill
ἀγαπᾶτε	pres	act	ind impv subj	2nd	n/a	pl	n/a	ἀγαπάω	you (pl) love (you pl) love! you (pl) may love
φάγοι	aor	act	opt	3rd	n/a	sg	n/a	ἐσθίω	may he/she/it eat
ἠδυνήθημεν	aor	pass	ind	1st	n/a	pl	n/a	δύναμαι	we were able
ποιήσω	aor fut	act	subj ind	1st	n/a	sg	n/a	ποιέω	I would do I will do
εὕροιεν	aor	act	opt	3rd	n/a	pl	n/a	εὑρίσκω	may they find
ἐπερίσσευον	impf	act	ind	1st 3rd	n/a	sg pl	n/a	περισσεύω	I was abounding they were abounding
ἔχοι	pres	act	opt	3rd	n/a	sg	n/a	ἔχω	may he/she/it have
πρόσευξαι	aor	mid	impv	2nd	n/a	sg	n/a	προσεύχομαι	you (sg) pray!
παθοῦσα	aor	act	ptc	n/a	nom	sg	fem	πάσχω	one (fem) who suffered suffering

Additional Notes:

- If you thought that πληρώσαι could also have been an aorist active infinitive, you were very close! The indicative form is πληρῶσαι.

Translation

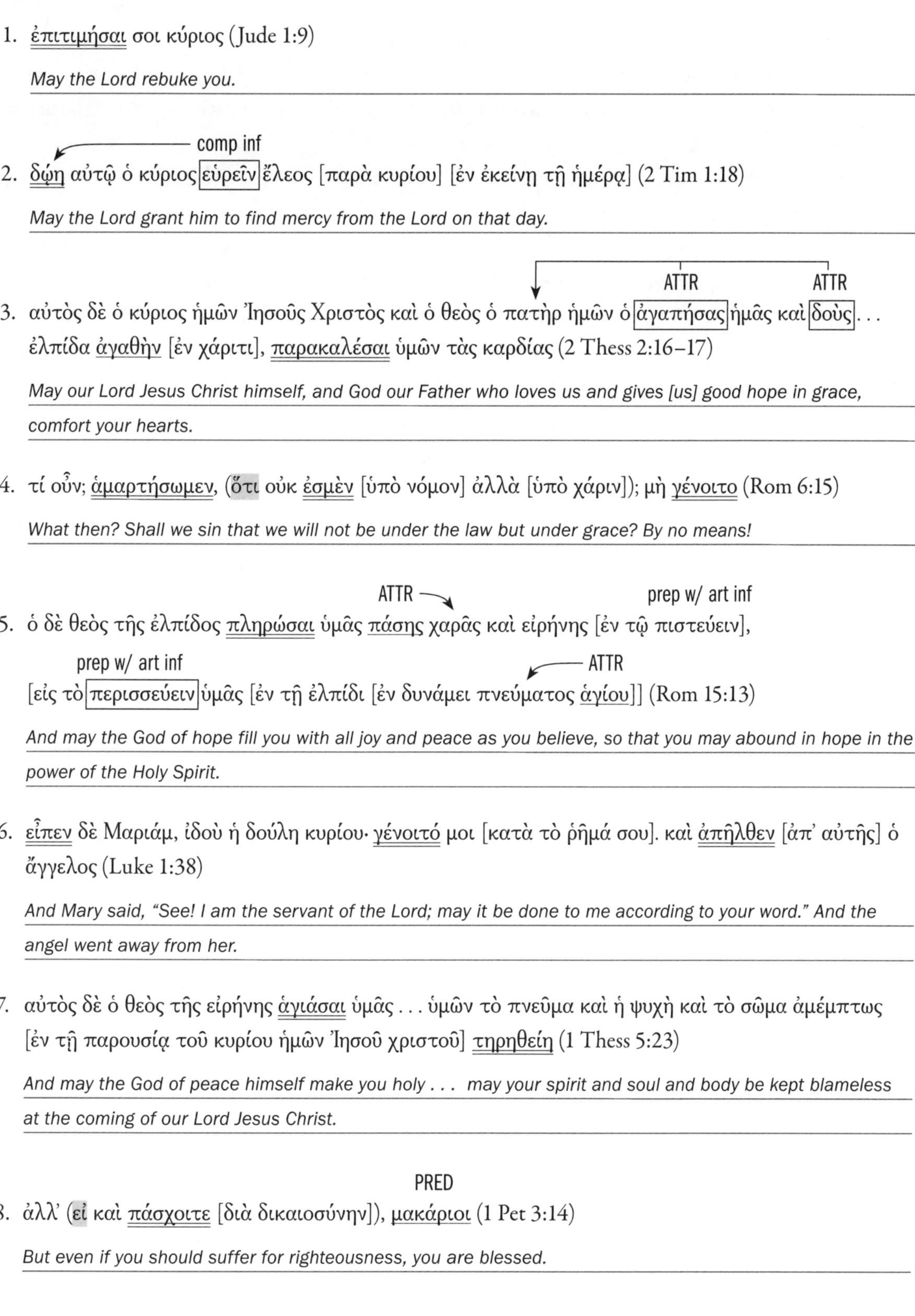

1. ἐπιτιμήσαι σοι κύριος (Jude 1:9)

   May the Lord rebuke you.

2. comp inf

   δῴη αὐτῷ ὁ κύριος εὑρεῖν ἔλεος [παρὰ κυρίου] [ἐν ἐκείνῃ τῇ ἡμέρᾳ] (2 Tim 1:18)

   May the Lord grant him to find mercy from the Lord on that day.

3. ATTR ATTR

   αὐτὸς δὲ ὁ κύριος ἡμῶν Ἰησοῦς Χριστὸς καὶ ὁ θεὸς ὁ πατὴρ ἡμῶν ὁ ἀγαπήσας ἡμᾶς καὶ δοὺς . . . ἐλπίδα ἀγαθὴν [ἐν χάριτι], παρακαλέσαι ὑμῶν τὰς καρδίας (2 Thess 2:16–17)

   May our Lord Jesus Christ himself, and God our Father who loves us and gives [us] good hope in grace, comfort your hearts.

4. τί οὖν; ἁμαρτήσωμεν, (ὅτι οὐκ ἐσμὲν [ὑπὸ νόμον] ἀλλὰ [ὑπὸ χάριν]); μὴ γένοιτο (Rom 6:15)

   What then? Shall we sin that we will not be under the law but under grace? By no means!

5. ATTR prep w/ art inf

   ὁ δὲ θεὸς τῆς ἐλπίδος πληρώσαι ὑμᾶς πάσης χαρᾶς καὶ εἰρήνης [ἐν τῷ πιστεύειν],

   prep w/ art inf ATTR

   [εἰς τὸ περισσεύειν ὑμᾶς [ἐν τῇ ἐλπίδι [ἐν δυνάμει πνεύματος ἁγίου]] (Rom 15:13)

   And may the God of hope fill you with all joy and peace as you believe, so that you may abound in hope in the power of the Holy Spirit.

6. εἶπεν δὲ Μαριάμ, ἰδοὺ ἡ δούλη κυρίου· γένοιτό μοι [κατὰ τὸ ῥῆμά σου]. καὶ ἀπῆλθεν [ἀπ᾽ αὐτῆς] ὁ ἄγγελος (Luke 1:38)

   And Mary said, "See! I am the servant of the Lord; may it be done to me according to your word." And the angel went away from her.

7. αὐτὸς δὲ ὁ θεὸς τῆς εἰρήνης ἁγιάσαι ὑμᾶς . . . ὑμῶν τὸ πνεῦμα καὶ ἡ ψυχὴ καὶ τὸ σῶμα ἀμέμπτως [ἐν τῇ παρουσίᾳ τοῦ κυρίου ἡμῶν Ἰησοῦ χριστοῦ] τηρηθείη (1 Thess 5:23)

   And may the God of peace himself make you holy . . . may your spirit and soul and body be kept blameless at the coming of our Lord Jesus Christ.

8. PRED

   ἀλλ᾽ (εἰ καὶ πάσχοιτε [διὰ δικαιοσύνην]), μακάριοι (1 Pet 3:14)

   But even if you should suffer for righteousness, you are blessed.

Additional Notes:

- Sentence 1 is a clear example of the importance of cases, not word order, in Greek. The subject is clearly κύριος, and σοι functions as the object. The verb ἐπιτιμάω often takes an object in the dative case. In case you are wondering, this is part of Jude's comment about Michael arguing with the devil over the body of Moses. Not even the archangel Michael would engage the devil directly, but instead he uttered this prayer.
- A few comments about the verbs in sentence 2. You may be used to translating forms of δίδωμι with the verb "to give" in English, but this Greek verb has a wide semantic range. In this verse, the English "grant" better renders δῴη. The dative αὐτῷ is best understood as an indirect object of δῴη, with the direct object left unexpressed: "May the Lord grant . . . to him." At the same time, however, αὐτῷ is also indicating the subject of the infinitive εὑρεῖν; clearly the Lord is not the one who is to find mercy! Some English versions translate this as follows: "May the Lord grant to him to find . . ." The translation, "May the Lord grant him to find . . ." is more natural English, however.
- Sometimes benedictions and prayers can be hard to translate because the verb often comes well after the subject (or subjects, in the case of sentence 3!). As always, the key is to identify the finite verbs and major syntactic units. Once you identify the two subjects in sentence 3, the rest of the sentence is straightforward. Finally, notice the use of personal pronouns in this blessing. First-person personal pronouns stress the common bond between Paul and the Thessalonians, namely, their shared union with the Father through Jesus Christ.
- Notice the deliberative subjunctive ἁμαρτήσωμεν in sentence 4. The ὅτι clause is functioning causally in this verse.
- The use of μὴ γένοιτο in sentence 4 (Rom 6:15) is a classic Pauline expression. This expression forbids even the possibility suggested by the deliberative subjunctive.
- Sentence 5 provides two good examples of an articular infinitive as the object of a preposition. The first construction, ἐν τῷ πιστεύειν, indicates contemporaneous time, which we've brought out with "as you believe." Remember that these expressions (as with many others) cannot be translated word for word into English. Moreover, the infinitive must often be rendered with a finite verb in English. This is also true for the next such construction, εἰς τὸ περισσεύειν ὑμᾶς. This construction indicates purpose and provides the "subject" of the infinitive: "So that you might abound." The use of "so that" in English requires the use of the English subjunctive, "you might." Notice also that there are two prepositional phrases, ἐν τῇ ἐλπίδι and ἐν δυνάμει πνεύματος ἁγίου, that are embedded in the εἰς τὸ περισσεύειν ὑμᾶς construction. Isn't Greek fun?
- The overall syntax of sentence 6 (Luke 1:38) is straightforward. Mary's faith, however, is staggering.

chapter TWENTY-SEVEN

OUTLINING NEW TESTAMENT PASSAGES: *Structural and Narrative Outlines*

Here is the text that is used as an example in the textbook if you want to mark as you work through the example.

Διὸ ἀναζωσάμενοι τὰς ὀσφύας τῆς διανοίας ὑμῶν νήφοντες τελείως ἐλπίσατε

ἐπὶ τὴν φερομένην ὑμῖν χάριν ἐν ἀποκαλύψει Ἰησοῦ Χριστοῦ

Here is a practice text. Working through the instructions in the textbook, use this text to write out a structural outline. The answer key is on the next page.

πορευθέντες οὖν μαθητεύσατε πάντα τὰ ἔθνη, βαπτίζοντες αὐτοὺς εἰς τὸ ὄνομα τοῦ πατρὸς καὶ

τοῦ υἱοῦ καὶ τοῦ ἁγίου πνεύματος, διδάσκοντες αὐτοὺς τηρεῖν πάντα ὅσα ἐνετειλάμην ὑμῖν· καὶ

ἰδοὺ ἐγὼ μεθ' ὑμῶν εἰμι πάσας τὰς ἡμέρας ἕως τῆς συντελείας τοῦ αἰῶνος.

Pop-Up Lexicon

ἀναζώννυμι	I bind up
ἀποκάλυψις, -εως, ἡ	revelation
διάνοια, -ας, ἡ	mind
ἐντέλλομαι	I command, I order
μαθητεύω	I make a disciple of
νήφω	I am sober, I am self-controlled
ὀσφῦς, -ύος, ἡ	waist, loins
συντέλεια, -ας, ἡ	end
τελείως	fully, completely

This text is Matthew 28:19–20. Did you come up with the following? Remember that an ellipsis indicates that the word order has been adjusted slightly.

19 οὖν
πορευθέντες . . .
μαθητεύσατε πάντα τὰ ἔθνη,
βαπτίζοντες αὐτοὺς
εἰς τὸ ὄνομα τοῦ πατρὸς καὶ
τοῦ υἱοῦ καὶ
τοῦ ἁγίου πνεύματος,
20 διδάσκοντες αὐτοὺς
τηρεῖν πάντα
ὅσα ἐνετειλάμην ὑμῖν·
καὶ ἰδοὺ
ἐγὼ εἰμι
μεθ' ὑμῶν . . .
πάσας τὰς ἡμέρας
ἕως τῆς συντελείας τοῦ αἰῶνος.

Alternatively, you may have come up with the following outline if you understood πορευθέντες as an attendant circumstance participle (which understands the participle as functioning parallel to the imperative):

19 οὖν
πορευθέντες . . .
μαθητεύσατε πάντα τὰ ἔθνη,
βαπτίζοντες αὐτοὺς
εἰς τὸ ὄνομα τοῦ πατρὸς καὶ
τοῦ υἱοῦ καὶ
τοῦ ἁγίου πνεύματος,
20 διδάσκοντες αὐτοὺς
τηρεῖν πάντα
ὅσα ἐνετειλάμην ὑμῖν·
καὶ ἰδοὺ
ἐγὼ εἰμι
μεθ' ὑμῶν . . .
πάσας τὰς ἡμέρας
ἕως τῆς συντελείας τοῦ αἰῶνος.

chapter TWENTY-EIGHT

TEXT FOR INTEGRATION

You can make a copy of this text to accompany your work on the integration exercises for chapter 28 in the textbook. In anticipation of your future Greek studies, the Pop-Up Lexicon is no longer available. Instead, all the words in this passage that have not yet been assigned as vocabulary are listed in the lexicon in the textbook. This will give you good practice for looking inflected words in a lexicon. Think of this as taking the training wheels off, because you are now ready to ride your bike all by yourself!

1. Δικαιωθέντες οὖν ἐκ πίστεως εἰρήνην ἔχομεν πρὸς τὸν θεὸν διὰ τοῦ κυρίου ἡμῶν

2. Ἰησοῦ Χριστοῦ δι᾽ οὗ καὶ τὴν προσαγωγὴν ἐσχήκαμεν τῇ πίστει[1] εἰς τὴν χάριν ταύτην

3. ἐν ᾗ ἑστήκαμεν καὶ καυχώμεθα ἐπ᾽ ἐλπίδι τῆς δόξης τοῦ θεοῦ. οὐ μόνον δέ,

4. ἀλλὰ καὶ καυχώμεθα ἐν ταῖς θλίψεσιν, εἰδότες ὅτι ἡ θλῖψις ὑπομονὴν κατεργάζεται,

5. ἡ δὲ ὑπομονὴ δοκιμήν, ἡ δὲ δοκιμὴ ἐλπίδα. ἡ δὲ ἐλπὶς οὐ καταισχύνει,

6. ὅτι ἡ ἀγάπη τοῦ θεοῦ ἐκκέχυται ἐν ταῖς καρδίαις ἡμῶν διὰ πνεύματος ἁγίου τοῦ δοθέντος

1. The Nestle-Aland 28 has square brackets around τῇ πίστει to indicate a textual conjecture. You will learn more about this in your exegesis classes. We have included these words in this text without square brackets so as to avoid any confusion with marking the text for syntax.

7. ἡμῖν. Ἔτι γὰρ Χριστὸς ὄντων ἡμῶν ἀσθενῶν ἔτι κατὰ καιρὸν ὑπὲρ ἀσεβῶν ἀπέθανεν.

8. μόλις γὰρ ὑπὲρ δικαίου τις ἀποθανεῖται· ὑπὲρ γὰρ τοῦ ἀγαθοῦ τάχα τις

9. καὶ τολμᾷ ἀποθανεῖν· συνίστησιν δὲ τὴν ἑαυτοῦ ἀγάπην εἰς ἡμᾶς ὁ θεός,

10. ὅτι ἔτι ἁμαρτωλῶν ὄντων ἡμῶν Χριστὸς ὑπὲρ ἡμῶν ἀπέθανεν.

11. πολλῷ οὖν μᾶλλον δικαιωθέντες νῦν ἐν τῷ αἵματι αὐτοῦ σωθησόμεθα δι᾽ αὐτοῦ

12. ἀπὸ τῆς ὀργῆς. εἰ γὰρ ἐχθροὶ ὄντες κατηλλάγημεν τῷ θεῷ

13. διὰ τοῦ θανάτου τοῦ υἱοῦ αὐτοῦ, πολλῷ μᾶλλον καταλλαγέντες σωθησόμεθα

14. ἐν τῇ ζωῇ αὐτοῦ· οὐ μόνον δέ, ἀλλὰ καὶ καυχώμενοι ἐν τῷ θεῷ

15. διὰ τοῦ κυρίου ἡμῶν Ἰησοῦ Χριστοῦ δι᾽ οὗ νῦν τὴν καταλλαγὴν ἐλάβομεν.

SCRIPTURE INDEX

Please note that many exercises are adaptations of actual Scripture citations—this is indicated by "cf." before the Scripture reference. As you progress through your studies, you should look up these references in a Greek New Testament and try to identify the adaptations and see how much of the actual text you can read. Students are encouraged to look them up in Barbara and Kurt Aland et al., eds., *Novum Testamentum Graece*, 28th ed. (Stuttgart: Deutsche Bibelgesellschaft, 2012).

ACTS

ROMANS

1 CORINTHIANS

2 CORINTHIANS

GALATIANS

EPHESIANS

1 THESSALONIANS

2 THESSALONIANS

2 TIMOTHY

HEBREWS

JAMES

1 PETER

1 JOHN

JUDE

REVELATION